Notice of Barr History.

✿ ✿ ✿

HOBOKEN, N. J.

The history and geneaology of the Barr Family beginning with Robert Barr, who came to this country from the North of Ireland with his five sons and one daughter in 1790, has been compiled by Rev. W. B. Barr of Hoboken, New Jersey.

The history covers eight generations of the Barr connection, which are a numerous family and scattered all over the United States. This is, and likely will be, the only history of the family that will ever be published. It is invaluable as a book of reference, and hence a copy of it should be in every family of the connection, and in every reference library in this country. (A number have already been purchased by historical and reference libraries.)

The *New York Genealogical and Biographical Record* for July 1901, says of this history: "The history traces the family through all their descendants to the latest child. The most interesting part of this book is the language in which the story is told—sprightly, eloquent, original. The volume is well printed, well illustrated, and thoroughly indexed."

It is 12 mo., cloth, pp. 216. The price is $2.00 a copy.

✿ ✿ ✿

The writer of it has a very few copies left which he wishes to dispose of. The book is worth double the money asked for it.

W. B. BARR.

Hoboken N. J.

Rev. W. B. Barr.

HISTORY

OF THE

BARR FAMILY,

BEGINNING WITH
GREAT-GRANDFATHER

ROBERT BARR,

AND

MARY WILLS;

THEIR DECENDANTS
DOWN TO THE LATEST
CHILD. . . . .

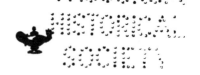

BY

REV. WM. B. BARR,

Pastor of First United Presbyterian Church

OF HOBOKEN, N. J.

1901.

PREFACE.

WHY write a Family History? What is the necessity for it? If it is deemed necessary to write up the pedigree of certain animals (beasts that perish), and register them, is not the record of a worthy family much more important?

God has set the solitary in families, and hence it is a divine institution.

If it is important that the church and the state should keep a careful record of their historical incidents and facts, it is equally so that the family, the most important of the three, should do so, because it lies at the foundation of the others. It is a well recognized fact that the prosperity of the state and the success of the church are dependent upon the virtue, good order and sanctity of the home. It is a pity that the power of the home for good or evil is so little recognized. Break down the safeguards of this, the first institution in the plan of God, and social order is destroyed and national greatness imperiled.

Again, "Blood is thicker than water." Hence those of the same family should be nearer and dearer to us than others, and we should be more interested in their success and welfare. The man who talks against his native place is unworthy to be known as one of its sons. And it has been well said, "They who care not to know their ancestors, are wanting in natural affection, and regardless of filial duty."

It certainly is a matter of vital importance to the members of a large family such as ours, as the country gets older, and the connection increases, and the name becomes more familiar in all the professions and trades, to be able easily to trace the family back to the early history of the country, when neighbors were few and far apart and the country was a trackless wilderness. Also, it is a great satisfaction and comfort for anybody who has any interest in his family connection to be able readily to place the name of any person or family, and to know who his ancestors were and to what branch of the great family he belongs, and how he stands related to every other member of the family. Many have given little attention to such matters, and hence are quite ignorant of their ancestors, or even their nearest relatives. To such persons a family history where such information can be had at a glance, would be a source of great pleasure.

In preparing such a history we have spared no pains to have it as complete and perfect as possible. Few have any conception of the labor, patience, perseverance, and sacrifice of time and money, necessary to gather up the history of a family scattered from Plymouth Rock to Golden Gate, and from Alaska to South America, over so great a country Some have not been able to see the importance of such a work, and hence were not careful to answer our correspondence, or to tell us what they knew. (We are happy to say these were few in number.) Others have been most accommodating and kind, giving valuable help and much encouragement in the work. We have no word of censure for any, but specially wish to return thanks to those who took pleasure in assisting us.

The writer became much interested in the matter of a family history some ten years ago, and realizing its importance to the generations that should follow, and knowing also the difficulty, if not impossibility, of gathering the history of our ancestors after a few of the older members now living should pass away, decided to complete the work at whatever cost. We feel repaid for the effort in the new acquaintances we have formed, and the information we have gathered about the connection, which is a great satisfaction to us; and we trust it will be as much so to those who shall avail themselves of a copy.

PREFACE.

We are only sorry that we cannot give a more complete history of this branch of the great BARR family, for doubtless there will be found many omissions and not a few mistakes, notwithstanding our effort to have it complete. But the best has been done that could be under the circumstances.

We send it forth, feeling that the best of motives have prompted us in compiling it, at a time when our life was so busy with the Master's work, and praying that it may be a blessing and comfort, as well as of information and inspiration to our numerous relatives and friends.

We might add that regrets have been sent by representatives of other branches of the Barr family, that we were not writing up the whole family. But the undertaking would be a vast one, requiring several volumes, which the writer had neither the time nor the disposition to undertake. The Barr's were among the very early settlers of the country. Old Fort Duquesne was located in a house owned by a Mr. Barr in 1742. Two of them were officers under General Washington in the struggle of the Colonial War. It would be a very interesting history. We hope some one will be inspired to undertake it.

INTRODUCTION.

IT is interesting to know the origin and morale of a family; the religious convictions, the genius, the thrift, the habits, and the crowning motives that actuated them; what they lived for and what they accomplished.

This much may be said: that so far as our research goes, we have not found or known of a member of the immediate connection that was ever in jail; that was wanting in industrious habits; or that was engaged in any dishonorable or disreputable business.

Our people are of Scotch-Irish descent; good Psalm-singing Presbyterian stock down through several generations, and it is a rare exception to find any of them in any other than a Presbyterian fold to-day. They are a religious family by natural generation, and we trust by spiritual regeneration. Our paternal ancestors were refugees in North Ireland from Scotland, under the Queen Ann persecution. They were Huguenots from France to Scotland, and were originally of Gallic or Celtic origin, as the name *Barre* (as originally spelled) implies.

As to the meaning of the name, the Arab word *Barr* means "wheat;" the Persian means "fruit;" the Irish word *Bar* means "excellence," which is Gilbair (bar), Anglicized Barr or Barre; the Hebrew word *Baar* means "was famous;" so the name in almost any language has a good meaning, and the people who bear it we trust are worthy of so good a name.

Our ancestors came to this country in moderate circumstances. They were for the most part tillers of the soil. They settled in the great forests of Pennsylvania; put up their own log cabins and hewed out their own farms. They gathered about their table many "olive plants," and on their table many comforts. They raised the flax, the wool and the leather, and made their own clothes and shoes. Railroads were not thought of, and farm machinery they had none, making it difficult to market what they had raised by the dint of hard toil.

They were not given to push themselves much into public notice. In political matters they preferred others above themselves, and hence few sought official position, although several have become ministers, doctors, lawyers, judges and legislators. Nevertheless, they were patriotic and loyal to their country and to their church. Several gave their lives on the side of the Union during our Civil War. This sounds like rather much self-praise, but we simply state facts which will be verified as we proceed with the history.

We have no reason to be ashamed of our crowd or our creed. The greatest legacy a parent can leave to a child is not farms, corner lots, bank stock, silver or gold, but a legacy of prayer and piety, a godly example and a true life. This richest inheritance has been transmitted as a family heirloom from father to son through many generations. Our ancestors were careful to lay the foundation of a religious life deep and broad in their children by wholesome Christian instruction, attendance upon the public ordinances of God's house, and the private means of grace. They were very careful in their observance of the Sabbath, temperate in their lives, and generally honest and upright in their dealings.

It is much to be well born, and it remains for us and our children to ever keep untarnished, and so preserve inviolable the character and good name of our glorious ancestors, and transmit it to coming generations.

NOTE.—The little figure to the right of a name indicates the generation to which the person belongs, beginning with Robert Barr as the first. This is necessary, owing to the repetition of names in the connecti on.

GREAT-GRANDFATHER
ROBERT BARR.[1]

Our Great-grandfather BARR's name was ROBERT.[1] Of him we do not know as much as we wish we did, and are sorry that it did not occur to ourselves, or some other member of the connection, to write such a history twenty-five or thirty years ago, when some of those now dead could have given us much interesting information about him.

He was born and lived in Donegal County, Ireland, near Coleraine. The place which he sold when he came to America, and where he lived and raised his family, and which was known as the "old Barr homestead," had been (as grandfather states in his memoirs) in the connection a great many years.

We have no account of his father's name or that of any of his brothers or sisters. We judge that he was born about 1725 or 1726 from all that we are able to gather. He married Miss MARY WILLS about 1747. She was a sister of Samuel Wills, who resided in Mifflin County, Pennsylvania, at the time they came to this country.

He was a devout worshiper of the true God, and brought up his family so that they "walked in the way of their father and in the way of their mother all the days of their lives."

His family consisted of—

ROBERT BARR.[2]   (Family I.)

DAVID BARR.[2]   (Family II.)

WILLIAM BARR [2]   (Family III)

SAMUEL BARR.[2]   (Family IV.)

GABRIEL BARR.[2]   (Family V.)

MARGARET BARR[2](or Peggy, as she was called). (Family VI.)

We are fortunate in getting possession of the memoirs of my grandfather, written in 1789, before they left Ireland, as well as on their journey across the ocean and after landing in this country. This book is ledger shape, bound by himself in deerskin, and written in a very legible hand. As few of the connection even know of this book, let alone any of its contents, we will take the liberty of quoting extensively from it for the information it contains, which will be interesting to those who never saw it. It is a great relic and much prized in the connection.

ROBERT BARR[1] left Ireland for America with his wife and family—except two sons, Robert and David, who preceded the family some years before—July 26, 1790, and got his first glimpse of America, Sabbath, October 3, 1790. They dropped anchor at New Castle, below Philadelphia, between three and four o'clock in the morning, and were exceeding glad not only to see land again, but to set foot on the country of their future home. My grandfather remarks: "That Sabbath day when the pilot came on board was a day of glad tidings. My heart filled so full I could not speak a word. How joyful is every one, but how few are praising God for his goodness. The first sight I have got of America is two little bunches of trees very like the rough Firth of Newtown, Lamavady."

Speaking of New Castle, on the Delaware, he says: "It has a handsome appearance. I think they would hardly deserve to live, who could not be satisfied to live in such a place.

"Wednesday, October 6th. We were taking a view of the country about New Castle. It is a place of great abundance of fruit of all sorts.

"Thursday, October 7th. We sailed from New Castle for Philadelphia and had a pleasant view of the country about Wilmington. It is very beautiful.

"Friday, October 8th. We weighed anchor one and a half miles from the city. It is the largest and most beautiful city I ever saw, and has the best situation for shipping."

If he thought so a century ago, what would he think to-day?

"On Monday, October 11th, we unshipped our goods, and engaged with Benjamin Blythe to haul our goods and my father and mother and sister for four guineas and a half.

"On Tuesday we were prepared to take our journey to Kishacoquillas Valley. Brother William has no wagon yet to haul his stuff. This is a sore trial as I have experienced, to leave him behind in such a situation and without our help. The roads are terrible—the worst I ever saw; wet and deep. The poor creatures are hauling and sweating and foaming. The first day we made eleven miles; the next day only ten miles, as it was very wet.

"Friday night we lodged at Peter Shoop's, above Lancaster. The next day (Sabbath) we made twelve miles."

He speaks of it as "another ill-spent Sabbath." They met that evening an Indian king and six of a company. They had jewels in their noses and ears.

When they came to Chambers Ferry, where they lodged on Monday evening, October 18th, they saw a boat going down the river with wheat, and they hailed her and bargained with those who had her in charge to take them and their goods to Oldtown (or Lewistown), Mifflin County, Pennsylvania.

Wednesday, October 20th, they reached Harrisburg, and the next day they left for Oldtown, arriving there Sabbath, October 24th.

Grandfather states; "The next day Gabriel and I went in search of Robert and David, the two brothers who had preceded us. We first came to David's house and found him and his son threshing wheat. We began to talk about the plantation. He knew us not, nor did he suspect us. After awhile we made ourselves known. This was a joyful meeting. Afterward we went to see Robert. He likewise was ignorant of us. Thus have we surprised them both with good news.

"Tuesday, October 26th. Robert, David, and Uncle Samuel Wills went to Lewistown to see daddy and mammy (as they say here), and they had a happy meeting.

"Wednesday, October 27th. This day they have brought father and mother and brother William and his wife and children up to brother David's house. These are happy days."

He says: "My father took that place where Frederick Baum lately lived. He (Baum) was buried in Lewistown the same Sabbath evening we landed there."

Now let us go back a little in our account of the family to the time of leaving the old home and native country. It was a great undertaking in those days to cross the ocean. Their vessels were sailing vessels, and they were dependent upon the wind and weather conditions. Our friends were thirteen weeks in crossing, which was a long time to be tossed upon the billows, while now we cover the distance by steam in a little over five days. It required considerable courage to brave the ocean voyage a century ago. To cross the ocean once meant that in all human probability they would never recross it.

To say good-bye to friends and native shores meant never to see them again. To break away from familiar faces and familiar scenes and familiar friends, meant the risk of not finding as good again and of becoming homesick to return without opportunity of gratifying their wish.

The account of the farewell to the old church and pastor is touching. Grandfather says: "June 6, 1790, I went to hear Mr. McKenny preach, and to take my farewell of him in Ireland, for I do not expect to hear him preach again. The men of this sect are the best preachers in the land and they are the best practical Christians. They speak the truth in season and out of season. My soul has often been refreshed with their godly conversation."

The House.

On Saturday, February 6, 1790, my grandfather writes: " My father is at last come to a full resolution to go to America. In the morning he came to brother Gabriel and me in the barn, and said to me: 'You must go and draw the papers to advertise the auction of our farming utensils and some other things; we must now put off.' Said he, 'It looks as if there was a special hand of Providence in this; for all our endeavors to take land have still been abortive.' He is very dispirited and melancholy; scarcely able to eat; breaks out with heavy sighs, and groans. They would have a very hard heart who could not pity him, for he is in great trouble.

"Tuesday, February 16, 1790. This is the day set for the sale. A large number of people came from all parts of the country. Andrew Johnston is cant master. We have sold by auction a good part of our goods, which makes but little money —about eight pounds, eighteen shillings."

They immediately prepared for the journey, but were often disappointed because the vessel did not start where and when appointed. Even after they had gotten on the vessel and had started, there were frequent delays, and on account of a great storm they were driven back after a whole day's sail almost within sight of land. Such were the difficulties of traveling in those days. Who can say when we read of their trials that "the former days were better than these?"

Great-grandfather Barr bought a farm a few years after in Stone Valley, Huntingdon County, Pennsylvania, one half mile north of McAlevy's Fort. In 1796 he put up a two-story log-house, large and well built, which is still standing. It has has housed five generations of the Barr family. It has been weather-boarded by Joseph Barr, a great-grandson of Robert Barr, who still occupies the homestead with his mother, Martha Barr, widow of Uncle Daniel Barr, youngest son of Grand-father Samuel Barr,[2] who fell heir to the homestead. My father, James Barr, was deeded some forty acres of the homestead farm lying on the west. Gabriel Barr, my father's brother, was deeded the tan-house and saw-mill.

The will of Great-grandfather Barr (the old, original will) is in possession of Joseph Barr, and is as follows:

WILL OF ROBERT BARR.

September 7, 1802.

In the name of God the Father, Son and Holy Ghost. Amen.

I, Robert Barr, farmer, of East Baree Township, in Huntingdon County, Pennsylvania, being of sound judgment, but weak of body, and calling to mind the mortality of mankind, and that shortly I must put off this clay tabernacle in the firm faith of a glorious resurrection of the body unto life everlasting through our Lord Jesus, my only Saviour, in whom I trust, believing that through his blessed merits I shall be saved from all my sins, that are great and many, and be admitted into the favor of God and endless felicity in glory. Amen.

I do, by these presents, make my last Will and Testament: imprimis I bequeath my soul to God who gave it me, and my body to the dust to be interred as I see fit to direct. I bequeath my worldly goods which God of his goodness hath bestowed upon me in manner following, towit:

After the expense of a decent burial, I bequeath to Mary, my beloved wife, and to my son Samuel, all my movable property, goods and chattels, ordering my son Samuel to give his mother a free maintenance during her natural life. I bequeath to my son

Robert one dollar, and to his son Samuel ten dollars. I bequeath to my son David one dollar. I bequeath to my son William one dollar, and to his son Robert ten dollars. I bequeath to Mary Barr, widow of my son Gabriel, late deceased, and his children, one dollar. And I order my son Samuel, and Mary my wife, to pay all my lawful debts and to be my executors; and I do hereby disannull all other former testaments, wills and legacies, and executors by me in any way before named, willed and bequeathed, ratifying this and no other to be my last and only Will and Testament.

In witness whereof I have hereunto set my hand and seal this seventh day of September, one thousand eight hundred and two.

ROBERT BARR. { *L. S.* }

Signed, sealed, published, pronounced and declared by said Robert Barr as his last Will and Testament in the presence of us, who in his presence and in the presence of each other have hereunto subscribed our names.

Witnesses present:
William McAlavy,
William McAlavy, Jr.,
William Nickle.

Huntingdon County, ss.
On the twelfth day of April, 1808, before me, the subscriber, Register for the Probate of wills and granting letters of administration in and for the county of Huntingdon, personally came William

McAlavy, Jr., who being duly sworn, deposeth and saith that he was present and did see and hear the within named Robert Barr sign, seal, publish and declare the within instrument of writing as and for his last Will and Testament, and that at the time of signing he was of sane and disposing mind; and that he subscribed his name thereto as a witness in the testator's presence, and at his request and in the presence of William McAlavy and William Nickle, who also subscribed their names as witnesses.

Sworn and subscribed April 12, 1808.

Andrew Henderson.   *William McAlavy, Jr.*

Great-grandfather made his home with my grandfather, Samuel Barr, until his death, which was in 1808. The will was drawn up in 1802 and executed in 1808. So that he must have been about eighty-two years of age at his death. His body rests in the old burial ground on the old homestead, not over eighty rods from the buildings. There being few if any churches at that time, the burial places were not always in connection with the meeting house. This is the oldest cemetery in the valley. Persons killed by the Indians are buried there. It is on the top of the highest hill on the place, overlooking the entire farm and buildings, and the country on all sides for miles distant. It is situated in a grove of beautiful pines, and was surrounded by an iron fence, which has since been replaced by a wooden fence.

Many of the oldest settlers in the valley are resting there. Great-grandfather Barr and his wife, and Grandfather Samuel Barr and his wife are buried on the east side of the cemetery, looking east toward the old home buildings and east toward Mount Zion below, typical of Mount Zion above. There the angels guard their precious dust. Rest in peace till Jesus comes again.

FAMILY I.

ROBERT BARR.[2]

The eldest son of Great-grandfather Barr was ROBERT BARR,[2] who preceded the family to this country several years and settled in Mifflin County, Pennsylvania, not far from Reedsville, in Kishacoquillas Valley. The place was afterwards bought by his son William, and is now owned by Rhoda Taylor. It is a beautiful and very rich farming valley.

He was born August 1, 1748, and hence was forty-two years old when the rest of the family arrived. Not much is known of him, as no records of the family could be found. He died December 23, 1834, in his eighty-sixth year. He married Miss CHRISTIAN REED. There is no record of her birth or death. His family consisted of five sons and two daughters.

    I DAVID BARR.[3]
    II WILLIAM BARR.[3]
    III JOHN BARR.[3]
    IV JAMES BARR.[3]
    V ROBERT BARR.[3]
    VI ELIZABETH BARR.[3]
    VII MARY BARR.[3]

(See DAVID BARR,[3] Family II, page 55.)

I DAVID BARR.[3]

1 DAVID BARR[3] was born May 6, 1782, in Mifflin County, Pennsylvania. He lived with his father until he married. He then moved to a farm which he bought, about one mile west of McAlevy's Fort, Huntingdon County, Pennsylvania, adjoining my father's farm on the west. He was our nearest neighbor. Here all his family were born.

He married Miss MARY BROWN in 1806. She was the granddaughter of Alex Brown and the great-granddaughter of Colonel James Alexander of revolutionary fame, who served with distinction under Washington at Valley Forge. She was born in December, 1785, and died September 16, 1865, aged seventy-nine years. They sold the farm to Mr. Osborn, and moved to Alliance, Ohio, in 1845, where they both died. There were born to them eight children.

1 ROBERT R. BARR.[4]
2 ALEXANDER B. BARR.[4]
3 DAVID BARR.[4]
4 WILLIAM B. BARR.[4]
5 JAMES A. BARR.[4]
6 JOHN BARR.[4]
7 MARY JANE BARR.[4]
8 CHRISTINA R. BARR.[4]

1 ROBERT R. BARR.[4]

1 ROBERT R. BARR[4] was born June 20, 1807. He was married to ELIZA A. YOUNG, of Armstrong County, Pennsylvania. He was a school-teacher, a good scholar, and a fine penman. He went to the state of Ohio before the rest of the family, and served as a notary public for several years, and died in 1849. Their children were—

DANIEL BARR,[5] who is a photographer and lives in Houston, Texas.

MARY JANE BARR,[5] who went to California many years ago, and nothing is known of her or her family.

ELIZABETH BARR,[5] who died at the age of five years.

2 ALEXANDER B. BARR.[4]

2 ALEXANDER B. BARR[4] was born February 4, 1811. He married MINERVA BARR, October, 1864, and died October 4, 1895, in his eighty-fifth year.

Mrs. Christiana R. Oswalt.

(Page 24.)

They lived on the old Barr homestead, three miles from Alliance. They had four sons and one daughter.

DAVID R. BARR,[5] born October 14, 1867.

WILLIAM H. BARR,[5] born April 27, 1869. He was killed by a train December 2, 1896.

ALEXANDER B. BARR,[5] born March 23, 1871.

WINFIELD G. BARR,[5] born October 1, 1872.

MARY E. BARR,[5] born February 18, 1875. She is unmarried, and lives with her brothers.

3 DAVID BARR.[4]

3 DAVID BARR[4] was born February 27, 1815. He married MARGARET BELL. She was born November 25, 1816. They had three children, all of whom died young, excepting MARY E. BARR.

MARY E. BARR.[5]

MARY E. BARR,[5] who was born July 13, 1837, married EUGENE MOINET May 5, 1860, and lives one mile north of Maximo, Stark County, Ohio, where they have lived for forty years, and where all their children were born. Mr. Moinet was born April 11, 1835. There were born to them—

1 CHARLES ALEX MOINET.[6]

2 FRANK LOUIS MOINET.[6]

3 CELESTINE MOINET.[6]

4 MARGARET MAGDALINA MOINET.[6]

5 WILLIAM JOSEPH MOINET.[6]

6 MARY ELIZABETH MOINET.[6]

7 JOHN EUGENE MOINET.[6]

1 CHARLES A. MOINET.[6]

1 CHARLES A. MOINET[6] was born January 11, 1861, and

was married to AMEDA OSWALT January 11, 1882. To them were born two children.

MARY HAZEL MOINET,[7] born May 12, 1884.

PAUL EUGENE MOINET,[7] born February 20, 1887.

Charles A. Moinet was employed by the Pennsylvania Railway Company as brakeman for eleven years. When shifting in the yards at Wooster, Ohio, he was struck by a shed projecting over a car of grain, and was knocked to the ground. He was given medical attention at once, but it was discovered that his spine was broken. He was taken to his home at Alliance, Ohio, that evening. This was on March 11, 1890. It was thought for a while that he would recover, and he was taken to the West Pennsylvania Hospital, in Allegheny, Pennsylvania, but he got no better, and died June 27, 1890, and was buried at Maximo, Ohio, June 29, 1890.

2 FRANK L. MOINET.[6]

2 FRANK L. MOINET[6] was born August 5, 1863. He was married to BERTHA L. ROSTELLER July 1, 1884. To them was born one child.

CHARLES GROVER MOINET,[7] was born March 17, 1885. He is employed by the Cleveland, Lorain & Wheeling Railroad Company, as engineer. He has been with them for six years. His home is in Lorain, the county seat of Lorain County, Ohio.

3 CELESTINE MOINET.[6]

3 CELESTINE MOINET[6] was born July 20, 1865, and was married to Miss MAGGIE WOOLF July 12, 1893. To them were born two children.

CHARLES EDWARD MOINET,[7] September 20, 1895.

MARY LYDIA MOINET,[7] October 5, 1897.

Celestine Moinet was employed by the Louisville Block and Tile Company prior to his death. The men were working overtime, and as he was going home along the railroad track he was struck by a special train carrying President McKinley home from his mother's funeral. He was picked up and taken to Alliance, where he was prepared for burial, and was taken home the next day. This was December 14, 1897. He was buried at Maximo. He left a wife and two children, who are making their home with his father and mother, near Maximo.

When President McKinley heard of the accident, he was very sorry, and sent Mrs. Moinet one hundred dollars, with an expression of his sorrow and sympathy.

4 MARGARET MAGDALINA MOINET.[6]

4 MARGARET M. MOINET[6] was born February 2, 1867, and married Mr. EDWARD A. GUEITTAR May 12, 1890. They have no children. They reside at 401 N. Newton Street, Canton, Ohio Mr. Guiettar has been employed by the Dueber and Hambden Watch Works, of Canton, Ohio, for the past six years.

5 WILLIAM J. MOINET.[6]

5 WILLIAM J. MOINET[6] was born April 14, 1870. He was married to NORA DONAHOE June 4, 1895.

He follows plumbing as a trade, and at the present time is in partnership with Vesseriat, the firm being known as Vesseriat & Moinet, of Alliance, Ohio. They do steam and gas fitting and all kinds of plumbing, also handle bicycles, guns, ammunition, and fishing tackle.

6 MARY E. MOINET.[6]

6 MARY E. MOINET[6] was born April 14, 1873. She married MORRIS R. DAWLING June 23, 1896. To them were born two children.

PAUL EUGENE DAWLING[7] was born March 23, 1898.
JOSEPH PATRICK DAWLING[7] was born November 5, 1899.

Mr. and Mrs. Dawling reside at Wellsville, Columbiana County, Ohio. Mr. Dawling has been employed as train-dispatcher by the Pennsylvania Railway Company, on the Cleveland & Pittsburg division, for the past six years.

7 JOHN EUGENE MOINET.[6]

7 JOHN E. MOINET[6] was born March 20, 1875. He is single and is living at Canton, Ohio. He has been employed by a plumbing company for the past year.

4 WILLIAM B. BARR.[4]

4 WILLIAM B. BARR,[4] son of DAVID BARR,[3] was born February 4, 1818. He married ELIZABETH ALEXANDER, daughter of Hugh Alexander, in 1839. He is still living at Alliance, Ohio. He is eighty-two years of age, and the only one of that family living. He was married twice. He had seven children by the first wife, and six by the second.

1 CHRISTIAN BARR,[5] born in 1840, is unmarried.

2 MARY BARR[5] was born in 1842, married, and lives in Wisconsin.

3 DAVID BARR[5] was born in June, 1844, married, and died in Iowa. He had one child.

4 HUGH A. BARR[5] was born in 1845, died unmarried, August 9, 1885.

5 MINERVA BARR[5] was born in 1847.

6 WILLIAM BARR[5] was born in 1851, and died unmarried, August 12, 1886.

7 ELIZABETH BARR[5] was born in 1853, and died at the age of six years.

Mr. Barr married for his second wife MARY ANN HOOPER, October 31, 1856, and had the following children to this union:

1 LAFAYETTE BARR,[5] who was born March 27, 1857, was married on March 28, 1894, to INEZ S. CURTISS. They had one boy baby who died in infancy.

Mrs. Rose A. Tolmie.

(Page 25.)

2 MORDECAI M. BARR,[5] who was born December 18, 1859, died September 7, 1894.

3 HANNAH ANN BARR,[5] who was born January 9, 1861, was married January 1, 1896, to MEREDITH McCOY. No children. She died August 12, 1896.

4 BETSY JANE BARR,[5] who was born February 14, 1863, was married on October 28, 1899, to THORNTON NEIS-WONGER. They have one child, HAZEL M. NEISWONGER.[6] Their address is Marlboro, Stark County, Ohio.

5 JAMES BARR[5] was born November 2, 1864.

6 SHERIDAN BARR,[5] who was born October 22, 1866, was married August 23, 1892, to MARY BELLE LLEWELLEN. They have three children.

EARL BARR, born November 24, 1893.

NELLIE BARR, born May 3, 1896.

LEILA BARR, born May 23, 1900.

They live in Canton, Ohio, McKinley Avenue

5 JAMES A. BARR.[4]

5 JAMES A. BARR,[4] born December 13, 1819, married MARY GRANT. Their family consisted of—

THOMAS M. BARR.[5]

REES BARR.[5] Married HENSY SCOTT.

DAVID BARR.[5] Married MARY B. OSWALT.

All the family are thought to be dead, as nothing has been heard of them for many years.

6 JOHN A. BARR.[4]

6 JOHN A. BARR,[4] son of DAVID BARR,[3] was born February 1, 1822. Died in Marshall County, Indiana. He was a farmer and was unmarried.

7 MARY JANE BARR.[4]

7 MARY JANE BARR[4] was born December 27, 1824. She made her home with Alexander Brown Barr on the old David Barr homestead, near Alliance, Ohio. She never married.

8 CHRISTIANA R. BARR.[4]

8 CHRISTIANA R. BARR,[4] was born September 15, 1826. She was the youngest child of DAVID BARR.[3] She married GEORGE W. OSWALT January 1, 1849. He was born April 29, 1827. She was a very large woman and weighed at her death two hundred and thirty pounds. She died of paralysis at the age of sixty-seven. Her weight was against her. She was a well looking woman at death. She received the stroke August 4th, and never spoke again. She died August 30, 1893. She made her home with her daughter, Mrs. Tolmie, at Tiffin, Ohio, for some years before her death. Her home had been in Stark County, Ohio.

Mrs. Oswalt was a nurse at the Fairmount Children's Home for nine years, where she had charge of the infant department. She was a faithful member of the United Brethren Church for over thirty-two years, and lived an exemplary Christian life. She came with her parents to Ohio from Huntingdon County, Pennsylvania, in 1845. She was as kind a mother as ever lived, and her example of patience and trust in God can never be forgotten. Her children were as follows:

1 ROBERT R. OSWALT,[5] born July 22, 1850. In hospital for thirteen years.

2 MARY B. OSWALT.[5]

3 CHARLES H. OSWALT,[5] born September 11, 1856. Died December 9, 1860.

4 JACOB A. OSWALT.[5]

5 ROSE A. OSWALT.[5]

6 NANCY JANE OSWALT,[5] born July 17, 1862. Died June 15, 1863.

2 MARY B. OSWALT.[5]

2 MARY B. OSWALT[5] was born February 24, 1852, and married her cousin DAVID BARR (son of James A. Barr) July 7, 1869. She died in Witchita, Sedgwick County, Kansas, October 12, 1872. She had one daughter.

MARTHA ELLEN BARR,[6] born 1870, died September 18, 1871.

4 JACOB A. OSWALT.[5]

4 JACOB A. OSWALT,[5] born April 27, 1858, lives in Eldora, Iowa, and is in the real estate business. He is single.

5 ROSE A. OSWALT.[5]

5 ROSE A. OSWALT was born April 17, 1860, and was married March 4, 1880, to Mr. JAMES TOLMIE. She takes her size from her mother somewhat, and weighs one hundred and ninety pounds.

Mr. Tolmie was born December 14, 1857. He is a machinist by trade, and lives in Tiffin, Ohio, and owns his own house in a beautiful part of the city. He was born in Canada and came to United States when small. His parents came from Scotland and were Scotch Presbyterians.

Their family consists of four sons:

JAMES ARTHUR TOLMIE,[6] born February 2, 1883. He is possessed of a fine voice for music, and sings in the high-school quartet and glee club, and is also a member of the church choir.

GEORGE ANDREW TOLMIE[6] was born April 14, 1887, and died March 11, 1889.

CHARLES KIRKWOOD TOLMIE[6] was born December 18, 1888.

RAYMOND VALENTINE TOLMIE[6] was born February 14, 1891.

We are much indebted to Mrs. Tolmie for the great help she gave us in collecting the history of this entire family. She was most kind, and gave us much encouragement.

II WILLIAM BARR.[2]

2 WILLIAM BARR,[2] second son of ROBERT BARR,[2] was born March 17, 1791, in Mifflin County, Pennsylvania. He married JANE DAVIS, daughter of Samuel Davis, October 12, 1813. She was born December 24, 1794. She died June 10, 1865, and Mr. Barr died June 10, 1868. She was in her seventy-second year and he was seventy-seven years of age.

He acquired his education in the district schools, and remained with his father until he was twenty-four years of age. He then rented a farm in Brown Township, Mifflin County, Pennsylvania, and cultivated it for two years, after which he bought the old Barr homestead—now owned by Rhoda Taylor —and there he lived and farmed successfully until he reached his sixtieth year. He was a Whig in politics, a good and esteemed citizen, an earnest member of the East Kishacoquillas Presbyterian Church, and for years an elder in that church. The writer remembers of being at his home with his father (James Barr) when a boy, more than once, and always enjoyed stopping, for he got a good dinner, to which a growing boy with a biting appetite, after crossing the mountain from Stone Valley, did justice. His daughters, who kept house for their father after their mother's death, were model cooks and housekeepers. He lived near the foot of the mountain, not far from the road from Greenwood Furnace to Lewistown. It was a good farm and a pleasant home, and cousin William and wife were pleasant, kind and good people.

His family consisted of two sons and seven daughters, all born on the same farm.

1 CHRISTIANA BARR.[4]
2 JOHN DAVIS BARR.[4]
3 ROBERT BARR.[4]
4 ELIZABETH BARR.[4]

Mr. William Barr.

(Page 26.)

5 CATHERINE FOSTER BARR.[4]
6 MARY JANE BARR.[4]
7 NANCY DAVIS BARR.[4]
8 MARGARET BARR.[4]
9 MARTHA B. BARR.[4]

1 CHRISTIANA BARR.[4]

1 CHRISTIANA BARR,[4] born August 12, 1814, married JOHN OLIVER CAMPBELL, living in the valley near Belleville. They had a good farm and were pleasant, good people. She died September 29, 1892, leaving no family. He died October 29, 1889.

2 JOHN DAVIS BARR.[4]

2 JOHN DAVIS BARR[4] was born November 6, 1815. He married POLLY ANN CLARK February 18, 1841. She was a daughter of Ephraim and Ann McNitt Clark. They settled close to his father, on a farm near Barrville. They had one son.

WILLIAM REED BARR,[5] born November 17, 1841, died in the sixth year of his age, March 15, 1847.

Mr. Barr attended the district schools, and worked for his father until he was twenty-six years of age. He then farmed the homestead for six years. The ensuing nine years he spent on a rented farm. He purchased the John Byler farm of one hundred and ten acres, and then retired from farming. He was an elder in the Reedsville Presbyterian Church at the time of his death. He served one term as county auditor and was also county commissioner for a term.

Mr. Barr died May 28, 1898. His wife died February 19, 1895.

3 ROBERT BARR.[4]

3 ROBERT BARR[4] was born September 18, 1817. He married Miss MARY ANN McKAIG November 18, 1846. She

was born in Chester County, Pennsylvania. She is still living. They went west to Dakota, Stephenson County, Illinois, March 16, 1866, bought a farm, and lived on it till October 12, 1881, when they moved to the town of Dakota, where they resided until August 17, 1890, when he died. His widow still resides there and owns the home.

He was elected to the eldership of the Rock Run Presbyterian Church, and served in the session until the time of his death.

They have four sons and one daughter. The sons are all farmers. The children are as follows:

1 WILLIAM HUTCHISON BARR.[5]

2 LEMUEL COLMARY BARR.[5]

3 JAMES McKAIG BARR.[5]

4 EMMA BARR.[5]

5 HOWARD FOSTER BARR.[5]

1 WILLIAM HUTCHISON BARR.[5]

1 WILLIAM H. BARR[5] was born October 9, 1847, in Mifflin County, Pennsylvania. He was married to JANE MARTIN, of Center County, Pennsylvania, in Rock Run, October 29, 1868.

She was born August 26, 1842. She came west in the fall of 1865 and made her home with her uncle, and was married there.

They lived on a rented farm until 1873, when they moved to Montgomery County, Iowa, and bought them a farm, where they live at present. Mr. Barr is an elder in the Red Oak Presbyterian Church at present. They have four sons and two daughters. All the sons but William Reed Barr are at home. Their post-office is Elliott, Iowa.

1 JAMES ROBERT BARR,[6] born August 26, 1869, a farmer at home.

2 WILLIAM REED BARR,[6] born May 15, 1872.
3 ANNA MINERVA BARR,[6] born June 19, 1875.
4 GRACE ELIZABETH BARR,[6] born October 27, 1877.
5 JOHN DAVIS BARR,[6] born August 29, 1880.
6 CARL MARTIN BARR,[6] born August 22, 1883.

2 WILLIAM REED BARR.[6]

2 WILLIAM R. BARR,[6] the second son of WILLIAM H.
BARR was born May 15, 1872. He died near Pilot Grove,
Montgomery County, Iowa, August 19, 1895. He was hurt
by his team running away while driving down grade with a load
of hay. The ladders gave way, throwing him violently on the
horses and wagon tongue. The wagon passed over him, frac-
turing the inferior maxillary, and injuring his spine and lungs.
He was paralyzed from his shoulders down. All was done for
him that kind and loving hands and hearts could do, but after
twenty-eight days of suffering, which he bore heroically, he died
in Christian submission to the will of Providence, who doeth all
things well.

3 ANNA MINERVA BARR.[6]

3 ANNA M. BARR,[6] the oldest daughter of WILLIAM H.
BARR,[6] born June 19, 1875, in Montgomery County, Iowa, was
married to GEORGE MILLEDGE September 5, 1894, and has one
daughter.

ETHEL MARIE MILLEDGE,[7] born June, 1896.

Their address is Stennett, Iowa.

4 GRACE ELIZABETH BARR.[6]

4 GRACE E. BARR,[6] second daughter of WILLIAM H.
BARR, was born in Montgomery County, Iowa, October 27,
1877. She was married to FRED BARKER June 2, 1897. They
have one daughter.

ALMA LEILA BARKER,[7] born March 7, 1898.

Morton Mills, Iowa, is their post-office address.

2 LEMUEL COLMARY BARR.[5]

2 LEMUEL C. BARR[5] was born in Mifflin County, Pennsylvania, February 21, 1850. LEMUEL C. was the second son of ROBERT BARR.[4] He married MARIE J. JOHNSTON October 26, 1871. She was born February 26, 1852, in Illinois, near Dakota. They moved to Shelby County, Illinois, June 27, 1875. He is a Sabbath-school superintendent. They have two children.

   1 LOTTIE ANNA BARR,[6] born January 29, 1874.

   2 JOHN HARRY BARR,[6] born June 27, 1875, at Prairie Home, Shelby County, Illinois.

The parents returned to northern Illinois, where they farmed until the fall of 1878, when they moved to Elliott, Montgomery County, Iowa, and farmed there until a few years ago, when they moved to Sabetha, Kansas. He works in the agricultural house of that place.

The children are both married.

   1 LOTTIE BARR[6] married WILLIAM WRIGHT (born May 17, 1874), and had two children. The oldest died.

   2 JOHN H. BARR,[6] the second child of Lemuel Barr, married ELVIRA GAGE, and they have two children. They follow farming for a living. (See Supplement.)

3 JAMES McKAIG BARR.[5]

3 JAMES M. BARR,[5] the third son of ROBERT BARR,[4] was born in Mifflin County, Pennsylvania, December 5, 1851. He was married November 26, 1896, to IDA BUSHING. She was born September 1, 1873, near Coatsville, Pennsylvania. She came to Dakota, Illinois, from Maquota, Iowa, in 1892, with her mother and stepfather, who was a Reform minister. They had two children.

   JOHN ROBERT BARR,[6] born July 1, 1898, and died when he was two days old.

   HOWARD TAYLOR BARR,[6] born July 23, 1899.

Mr. Robert Barr.

(Page 27.)

They live on a rented farm near Dakota, Illinois. He is superintendent of a Sabbath-school.

4 EMMA BARR.[5]

4 EMMA BARR,[5] daughter of ROBERT BARR,[4] was born in Mifflin County, Pennsylvania, June 3, 1855. She is at home with her mother. They live in the village of Dakota, Illinois.

5 HOWARD FOSTER BARR.[5]

5 HOWARD F. BARR,[5] the youngest son of ROBERT BARR,[4] was born in Mifflin County, Pennsylvania, January 22, 1858. He was married to AMANDA WALKER March 24, 1881. She was born March 2, 1854. He went west in 1866, bought the old homestead owned by his father, and that is their home to-day.

They have seven sons and one daughter, all at home but the oldest, who works for his neighbor.

HOWARD IRWIN BARR,[6] born April 3, 1882.

EARL EVERETT BARR,[6] born August 2, 1884.

FLOYD WALKER BARR,[6] born July 24, 1886.

JAMES HERBERT BARR,[6] born October 6, 1888.

LESLIE TENNYSON BARR,[6] born March 1, 1891.

JOHN CULLEN BARR,[6] born April 10, 1893.

MARY EDITH BARR,[6] born December 23, 1895.

The last was an infant, born June 9, 1900.

The second son is the main standby on the farm. The third son, Floyd, is in his second year in the College of Northern Illinois.

4 ELIZABETH BARR.[4]

4 ELIZABETH BARR,[4] second daughter of WILLIAM BARR,[3] was born July 5, 1819, in Mifflin County, Pennsylvania. She married JOSEPH KYLE April 17, 1843. He died November, 1879. Mrs. Kyle died October 29, 1891.

Mr. Kyle was a farmer, and all his sons now living follow the same business. He was the son of Crawford Kyle, and was born, reared, and died (at the age of sixty-four) on his father's farm, along the back mountain road in Kishacoquillas Valley, Mifflin County, Pennsylvania.

To them were born three sons and one daughter.

1 CRAWFORD KYLE[5] was born March 30, 1844, and died August 19, 1845.

2 WILLIAM B. KYLE[5] was born July 14, 1846. Married MARY TAYLOR HENRY December 19, 1876. To them were born two children.

RHODA TAYLOR KYLE,[6] born January 18, 1883.

JOSEPH REED KYLE,[6] born April 21, 1885.

MR. W. B. KYLE farmed near Reedsville, Mifflin County, Pennsylvania. He died November, 1889.

3 ALLAN TAYLOR KYLE,[5] born August 6, 1848, married ELIZABETH MITCHELL, May, 1883. He died April 5, 1889.

4 JENNIE E. KYLE[5] was born July 13, 1852, and was married to REV. JOHN C. OLIVER May 23, 1878, by Rev. A. H. Parker, at Reedsville, Pennsylvania.

Rev. Oliver was born at Graysville, Huntingdon County, Pennsylvania, October 15, 1845. He was the eldest son of James and Margaret (Campbell) Oliver. Mrs. James Oliver was born in Mifflin County, Pennsylvania. They lived at Graysville for almost half a century. His parents were most estimable Christian people and highly esteemed.

Rev. Oliver prepared for college at Tuscarora Academy, Schuylkill County, Pennsylvania. He graduated at Princeton University in 1872, and at Princeton Theological Seminary in 1875. He was first honor man in the academy, where he was also an instructor. He was class president during his senior year at Princeton, also president of the Philadelphia society of Princeton. He was elected by college classes a life-member of the American Bible Society. While yet in the seminary he was called to be the pastor of Lower Chanceford Presbyterian Church, at Academia, Pennsylvania. After a pastorate of ten years he left that church with three hundred and forty members, to accept a call to Tidioute, in Warren County, Pennsylvania, where after two years his health failed and he resigned and spent a year traveling. Afterward he located at Latrobe, Pennsylvania, where he spent ten years as pastor and presbyterial missionary. During that time he was largely instrumental in starting six new churches in the bounds of Blairsville Presbytery. He is at present pastor of Long Run Church, at Circleville, in the suburbs of Pittsburg. In addition to his ministerial and pastoral duties, he is correspondent for several of the church papers, and an occasional contributor to several literary magazines.

Their family consists of—

BESSIE BARR OLIVER.[6]

MARGARET CAMPBELL OLIVER.[6]

Both are school-girls at Wilson College, at Chambersburg, Pennsylvania.

5 CATHERINE F. BARR.[4]

The third daughter of WILLIAM BARR[3] was CATHERINE FOSTER BARR.[4] She was born March 20, 1822. She married Mr. DAVID CUMMINS January 11, 1843.

Mr. Cummins, who was the second son of Colonel Cummins, of Mifflin County, Pennsylvania, went to California during the gold excitement, and came back after some years to Lake City, Minnesota, and made his home with his sons until his death, in 1873.

Mrs. Catherine Cummins kept house for her father several years previous to, and during his last illness. After his

death in 1868 she lived in Belleville for five or six years, and
then went to Stevenson County, Illinois, where her brother
Robert Barr and family, also two sisters (Nancy Stewart and
Mrs. Mary Jane Millikin) and families lived. Then she moved
to Lake City, Minnesota, in the spring of 1881, where her boys
had preceded her.

She was married there to Rev. NELSON MOON, November,
1883. He had been a local preacher in the M. E. Church for
fifty years and owned a farm of one hundred and sixty acres in
Bear Valley, which with the help of his sons, he farmed for
several years. He had a family of four sons and one daughter.
One son died of fever during the Rebellion. Two of his boys
live in Texas, and OWEN, the other son, and his family live in
Big Stone County, Minnesota.

Mr and Mrs. Moon bought their own home after
their marriage in Lake City—a beautiful city of between three
and four thousand inhabitants—and have resided there ever
since. Mr. Moon is past eighty-two, but leads an active
life and is interested in every good work. Mrs. Moon is
practically an invalid and feeling the infirmity of years, but has
good hope of the world to come.

Mrs. Moon by her first husband had three sons.

1 WILLIAM STERRETT CUMMINS.[5]

2 HOWARD CUMMINS.[5]

3 JOHN D. CUMMINS.[5]

1 WILLIAM STERRETT CUMMINS.[5]

1 WILLIAM STERRETT CUMMINS,[5] born in Mifflin County,
Pennsylvania, October 11, 1843, enlisted in the Bucktail Regiment, in Huntingdon County, Pennsylvania, in 1861. He was
confined in Libby Prison for three weeks, and after escaping
was killed in the battle of South Mountain, Maryland, September
14, 1862.

Mrs. Jennie E. Oliver,   Rev. John C. Oliver,
Miss Bessie B. Oliver,
Miss Margaret C. Oliver.

(Page 32.)

2 HOWARD CUMMINS.[5]

2 Howard Cummins[5] was born September 8, 1845. He married Miss Emma J. Davis, daughter of William Davis. Her mother's maiden name was Mary M. Porter. Her parents were born and raised in Stone Valley, Huntingdon County, Pennsylvania, and were members of the United Presbyterian Church. Rev. J. M. Adair was their pastor. Emma was a fine-looking young lady, as we remember her, and a girl of good Christian principles, and has made a good wife and a kind, good mother.

They were married March 22, 1882. They moved to their present home near Beaver Creek, Minnesota, May 11, 1882. They are prosperous farmers in Rich County, Minnesota, two miles from Beaver Creek. They have five sons and one daughter.

Jessie Clair Cummins[6] was born July 19, 1883.

Elmer Foster Cummins[6] was born May 9, 1885.

William Irwin Cummins[6] was born April 20, 1887.

Roy Harrison Cummins[6] was born November 7, 1888.

Dwight Russel Cummins[6] was born December 17, 1893.

They believe in the sentiment of Horace Greeley: " Go West, young man," and grow up with the country.

3 JOHN D. CUMMINS.[5]

3 John Davis Cummins[6] was born April 28, 1847. He married Louisa Beatty October 13, 1870. Mr. Cummins has followed engineering mostly since his marriage. They are now living at Des Moines, Iowa. They have changed about some: from Lake City to Minneapolis; from there to Columbus, Ohio; then to Kentucky (where their son William Beatty Cummins remained); and then to Des Moines, where they now live. Mr. J. D. Cummins was three years in the Civil War, and escaped without a scratch.

They have three living children and several that died in infancy. The living are:

CARRIE MAY CUMMINS.[6]

WILLIAM BEATTY CUMMINS.[6]

EMMA RIGHLEY CUMMINS.[6]

6 MARY JANE BARR.[4]

1 MARY JANE BARR,[4] the fourth daughter of WILLIAM BARR,[3] was born July 12, 1824, in Mifflin County, Pennsylvania. She married R. M. MILLIKIN. He was an elder in the Rock Run Presbyterian Church. He died September 24, 1888. Mrs. Millikin died April 19, 1891, aged sixty-seven years, nine months, and six days. They had one son and three daughters.

HARRIS T. MILLIKIN[5] married NETTIE BEAVER. Mr. Millikin died January 27, 1896.

Since Harris's death the balance of the family have lived in a suburb of Chicago. Address, Edgewood, Illinois.

7 NANCY DAVIS BARR.[4]

7 NANCY D. BARR,[4] the fifth daughter of WILLIAM BARR,[3] was born January 4, 1827, in Mifflin County, Pennsylvania. She married JONATHAN STEWART. They moved West in 1852. He followed farming until the Civil War broke out, and then enlisted in the Seventy-fourth Illinois Regiment. He served almost three years. Since that time he has worked at the carpenter trade, but is not able to do hard work. He keeps some bees, and is able to attend to them; that is about the extent of his work. They have two daughters.

1 IDA OPHELIA STEWART.[5]

2 JENNIE DAVIS STEWART.[5]

1 IDA OPHELIA STEWART.[5]

1 IDA OPHELIA STEWART[5] was married to JOHN C. YOUNG, and lives near Freeport, Illinois. After their marriage

Mr. Young accepted a position as mail agent on the Illinois Central Railroad, which position he filled for almost twenty years. He was in three railroad wrecks, but unfortunately the last was too much for him. His spine was so badly injured that he gave up his position and is now a hopeless invalid. He is able to get around, but his physician says he can never be any better. They have three boys.

ARTHUR YOUNG.[6] He is a day laborer.

ROY YOUNG.[6] He is an up holster.

CLYDE YOUNG.[6] He is clerking in a store in Freeport.

2 JENNIE DAVIS STEWART.[5]

2 JENNIE D. STEWART[5] was married to ELIAS BAKER. He is a farmer and they live near Cockrell, Stephenson County, Illinois. They have two daughters and one son living. They spent part of their married life near White Rock, Kansas. While living there they lost two little girls: BERTIE,[6] aged eight years, and BESSIE,[6] aged six years.

MAUDIE,[6] the oldest daughter, is clerking in a drygoods store in Des Moines, Iowa. The youngest daughter, IDA,[6] is at home. The son helps on the farm. Mr. Baker is superintendent of a Sabbath-school near his place, and takes an interest in Christian work.

8 MARGARET BARR.[4]

8 MARGARET BARR,[4] the sixth daughter of WILLIAM BARR,[3] was born June 7, 1829, in Mifflin County, Pennsylvania. She was married to Mr. JOHN SHADLE, December 7, 1849. He was born April 22, 1816, and died June 18, 1889. His father's name was Henry Shadle. Mrs. Shadle died July 1, 1873, aged forty-four years and one month.

After marriage they went to housekeeping in part of his father's house. They lived there for twenty years, then moved to a farm which they purchased from Mr. James Millikin, two miles south-east of where they did live.

They had three children, two sons and a daughter.

1 Samuel Wilson Shadle.[5]

2 John Harvey Shadle.[5]

3 Annetta Jane Shadle.[5]

1 SAMUEL WILSON SHADLE.[5]

1 The oldest son, Samuel Wilson Shadle,[5] was born May 10, 1851, and died June 24, 1897. He prepared for college at Kishacoquillas Seminary, graduated at LaFayette College, and subsequently studied law at Lancaster, Pennsylvania.

2 JOHN HARVEY SHADLE.[5]

2 John Harvey Shadle[5] was born February 22, 1853. Died February 3, 1880, of typhoid fever.

3 ANNETTA J. SHADLE.[5]

Annetta Jane Shadle[5] was born September 16, 1855, and was married to Mr. Gruber H. Bell March 21, 1878. They had three children.

John Foster Bell[6] was born February 23, 1879, and is at present attending school at Dickinson Seminary, Williamsport, Pennsylvania.

Harvey Thompson Bell[6] was born June 19, 1884. He died June 18, 1890, of dyptheria.

Mary Barr Bell[6] was born April 15, 1890. She is at home.

Mr. Bell was in the legislature of Pennsylvania a term. He lives at 67 Logan Street, Lewistown, Pennsylvania.

9 MARTHA B. BARR.[4]

9 Martha B. Barr,[4] the seventh daughter of William Barr,[3] was born October 7, 1831, in Mifflin County, Pennsyl-

vania, and was married to Mr. ROBERT P. McCLAY November 25, 1857, by Rev. Ross Stephenson. They made their home in Mifflin County, Pennsylvania, near the place of their birth. They have two children.

1 WILLIAM BARR McCLAY,[5] born in 1860.

2 JANE LENDRUM McCLAY,[5] born January 3, 1865.

1 WILLIAM BARR McCLAY.[5]

1 WILLIAM B. McCLAY[5] married LIZZIE M. CAMPBELL, of Mifflin County, February 15, 1888. They have three children.

HELEN ARGYLE McCLAY,[6] born January 8, 1890.

RALPH ANDERSON McCLAY,[6] born June 26, 1891.

ROBERT BARR McCLAY,[6] born November 16, 1893.

2 JANE L. McCLAY.[5]

JANE L. McCLAY,[5] born January 3, 1865, married W. GEORGE WILSON, May 18, 1893. They have three children.

MARTHA BARR WILSON,[6] born November 5, 1894.

SARAH G. WILSON,[6] born July 3, 1898.

MAY McCLAY WILSON,[6] born September 4, 1899.

Mr. and Mrs. Wilson have their home in Belleville, Mifflin County, Pennsylvania.

Mr. Robert McClay was an elder in the West Kishaco-quillas Presbyterian Church for many years before his death, which occurred April 20, 1881, at the age of sixty-nine years and eleven months. Mrs. McClay is still living, and makes her home with her daughter at Belleville, Pennsylvania.

This closes quite a full account of a large family of children, grandchildren, and great-grandchildren of WILLIAM BARR,[3] all of whom, without exception, are most respectable; comfortably situated in life; and many of whom have been elders, Sabbath-school superintendents, and interested in and connected with some branch of the Church of Jesus Christ.

Mr. Barr and his wife have been dead many years, but his life and Christian influence are being reproduced a hundred-fold, and his soul goes marching on down the generations. What a lesson of responsibility is here taught every parent: viz., to live his or her best, and bring up a worthy family, so that the home altar fires may ever burn brightly for the Lord.

III JOHN BARR.[3]

3 JOHN BARR,[3] the third son of ROBERT BARR,[2] and grandson of ROBERT BARR,[1] was born in Mifflin County, not far from Reedsville, in 1793. He was an apprentice boy to Robert Gardner of Spruce Creek, Center County, Pennsylvania, and learned chair-making with him (and he made good ones). He had a hard struggle in his early life.

He married JEANETTE BORLAND, of Scotch descent. She was raised on Spruce Creek. They were married in 1808, and removed to East Branch, three miles south-east of McAlevy's Fort, Pennsylvania, on the farm now owned by my sister, Mrs. Wilson. There were born to them nine children.

 1 MARGARET BARR.[4]
 2 CHRISTIANA REED BARR.[4]
 3 NANCY BARR.[4]
 4 ELIZABETH BARR.[4]
 5 JOHN BARR.[4]
 6 MARTHA BARR.[4]
 7 HETTY BARR[4] } Twins.
 8 ROBERT BARR[4] }
 9 WILLIAM BARR,[4] born July 5, 1831. Died of scarlet fever when a baby.

1 MARGARET BARR.[4]

1 MARGARET BARR,[4] born March 13, 1809. Married DAVID SEMPLE May 4, 1830. Died in Adams County, Ohio·

2 CHRISTIANA REED BARR.[4]

2 CHRISTIANA REED BARR,[4] born December 13, 1812, and married JAMES SEMPLE April 14, 1835. He was a cousin of David Semple, who married the sister.

3 NANCY BARR.[4]

3 NANCY BARR[4] was born April 2, 1815. She never married, and died at the home of her sister, Mrs. Hettie Porter, January 30, 1886.

4 ELIZABETH BARR.[4]

4 ELIZABETH BARR,[4] born March 1, 1818, was married to ROBERT HUEY April 1, 1862, by Rev. Moses Floyd. She died April 5, 1867. To them was born one son, SAMUEL G. HUEY.

SAMUEL G. HUEY.[5]

Rev. SAMUEL G. HUEY[5] was born May 7, 1864, near McAlevy's Fort, Huntingdon County, Pennsylvania. He graduated at Westminster College, June 20, 1888, and at Allegheny Theological Seminary March 25, 1891. He was licensed by Mercer Presbytery, at West Middlesex, Pennsylvania, April 15, 1890; and was ordained and installed by the Presbytery of Wisconsin, as pastor of Rock Prairie congregation (where he still preaches) August 19, 1891. He has been quite successful in this, his only settlement, and enjoys the work.

He was married September 10, 1891, to Miss EVA F. DONALDSON, of New Wilmington, Pennsylvania, by Rev. J. M. Mealy, D. D. Her father's name was Zechariah Donaldson, who for many years was a prominent elder in the Neshannoch Presbyterian Church. He is a nephew of Rev. Alexander Donaldson, D. D., of Elders Ridge, Pennsylvania.

Their family consists of three daughters.

GRACE HUEY,[6] born December 29, 1894.

HELEN HUEY,[6] born October 27, 1896.

RUTH CRAWFORD HUEY,[6] born April 29, 1900.

Brother Huey is a genial, live, active man, up to date, and is succeeding admirably.

5 JOHN BARR.4

5 JOHN BARR4 was born May 14, 1820. He was married twice. His first wife was ANNA ELIZA BELL, born 1822, married May 19, 1844. She died May 7, 1849, and left two children, one a babe which soon followed the mother, born April 26, 1849, and died July 19, 1849. The other was ELIZABETH JANE.

ELIZABETH JANE BARR,5 born August 31, 1846, was married to LEMUEL MORRISON September 18, 1877, by Rev. W. A. Clippinger. Mr. and Mrs. Morrison moved to Tower Hill, Illinois, in the spring of 1884. They have one son CHARLIE, born September 1, 1878, who is clerking in a drygoods store in Lower Hill. Mr. Morrison is a farmer.

Mr. Barr married for his second wife MARY JANE PORTER, of Huntingdon County, Pennsylvania, November 9, 1851. To them were born nine children.

1 WILLIAM P. BARR.5

2 MARGARET S. BARR,5 is single, lives at home and teaches school.

3 ELLA M. BARR.5

4 ANNA N. BARR,5 single and at home.

5 KATE BARR,5 single and at home.

6 SARAH T. BARR,5 single and at home.

7 JOHN N. BARR,5 at home and unmarried.

8 ARCHIE BARR,5 at home.

9 MILLIE BARR.5

1 WILLIAM PORTER BARR.5

1 WILLIAM P. BARR,5 was born September 21, 1852, in Stone Valley, Huntingdon County, Pennsylvania. He married AGNES STEWART (daughter of Samuel Stewart), near McAlevy's

Rev. Samuel G. Huey.

(Page 41.)

Fort, Pennsylvania, July 24, 1873. She was born November 18, 1850. They moved from the valley February 25, 1887, to Clearfield County, Pennsylvania; and then to Center County, Pennsylvania, March 2, 1898. Their present address is Sandy Ridge, Pennsylvania. They have seven children.

ALMA B. BARR[6] was born September 10, 1874, in Huntingdon County, Pennsylvania.

WALTER M. BARR[6] was born March 8, 1877, in Huntingdon, County, Pennsylvania.

McCARL BARR[6] was born December 21, 1879, in Huntingdon County, Pennsylvania.

CLYDE BARR[6] was born May 19, 1882, in Huntingdon County, Pennsylvania.

MEAD BARR[6] was born July 28, 1884, in Huntingdon County, Pennsylvania.

ANNA MAUDE BARR[6] was born January 29, 1886, in Huntingdon County, Pennsylvania.

FRANK BARR[6] was born March 28, 1890, in Clearfield County, Pennsylvania.

Mr. W. P. Barr is an engineer at the Sandy Ridge Fire Brick Works, and his sons Walter, Carl and Clyde work at the same works. All are making good wages and doing well.

3 ELLA M. BARR.[5]

3 ELLA M. BARR,[5] born July 18, 1858, was married October 23, 1884, to THOMAS A. MAGILL (born June 9, 1859), by Rev. Adair, and lives near Irwin, Pennsylvania, east of Pittsburg. Their children are as follows:

JENNIE BLANCH MAGILL,[6] born November 2, 1885.

JAMES ARCHIE MAGILL,[6] born January 31, 1887.

VERNON T. MAGILL,[6] born February 26, 1889.

CHARLES T. MAGILL,[6] born April 23, 1891.

JOHN H. MAGILL,[6] born October 31, 1893.

DAVID R. MAGILL,[6] born May 23, 1895.
GEORGE A. MAGILL,[6] born September 13, 1897.
ALVIRA J. MAGILL,[6] born August 2, 1900.

9 MILLIE BARR.[5]

9 MILLIE BARR[5] was married to F. H. DUNLAP, of Mercer County, Pennsylvania, November 17, 1898. They live at Youngstown, Ohio, where they moved August 29, 1899. They have one son.

Frederick Harold,[6] born October 3, 1899.

Mr. Dunlap is foreman of the Enterprise Boiler Works, of Youngstown, Ohio. They are members of the Tabernacle United Presbyterian Church.

Mrs. John Barr[4] died August 21, 1879, of consumption, at her home in Stone Valley, in her fifty-third year, and was buried in the United Presbyterian Church burial ground. She was a kind-hearted woman, one of the best of mothers, and trained her large family up to industry, and in the fear of the Lord; and died in the hope of a glorious immortality.

Mr. John Barr[4] deserves more than a passing notice. He lived on a farm in the upper end of Stone Valley, not far from the foot of Broadtop Mountain. Mr. Barr and family made the United Presbyterian their church home, and were remarkably faithful in their attendance on church ordinances, for although fully four miles from the church, they were seldom absent, and they were a family that would be missed if they were absent.

Mr. Barr was a good-natured, jovial man, who enjoyed and could tell a good story. He was elected by the building committee of his church to superintend the erection of the beautiful and commodious two-story brick building. Owing to the fact that the kiln of brick was spoiled in the burning, it made much expense and trouble for Mr. Barr, as the facing brick had to be hauled from Huntingdon. But he showed his business tact and energy in the manner in which he succeeded. The work was approved by the building committee, and Mr. Barr was highly commended for the faithful manner in which he had attended to the business. He died March 21, 1888, a man that was very much missed in the church and community.

6 MARTHA BARR.[4]

6 MARTHA BARR[4] was born on the East Branch, near McAlevy's Fort, December 1, 1822. She was the sixth child of JOHN BARR.[3] She was married twice. First to JAMES PORTER, January 24, 1849, who died soon after. There were no children by the first husband.

She married for her second husband SAMUEL McCORD, March 4, 1851. They lived on a farm one and one-half miles west of McAlevy's Fort, Pennsylvania. Mr. McCord was not a rugged man and could not stand hard work. We could see him every day almost, passing our buildings to the fort. He was a kind man and a good neighbor. Mrs. McCord was a good manager and a hard-working woman. To them were born two daughters.

1 NANCY JANE McCORD.[5]
2 MARGARET McCORD.[5]

1 NANCY JANE McCORD.[5]

1 NANCY JANE McCORD[5] was born January 24, 1852, and was married to JAMES EWING February 17, 1876. They farm and own their own farm of one hundred and sixty acres, near Pontiac, Livingston County, Illinois. They moved to their present home March 1, 1876. They have six children, all living.

GRACE M. EWING[6] was born November 4, 1876.

FANNIE M. EWING[6] was born August 20, 1878.

WILLIAM M. EWING[6] was born October 29, 1879.

CARRIE M. EWING[6] was born August 27, 1881.

JAMES H. EWING[6] was born March 20, 1883.

ROBERT G. EWING[6] was born September 14, 1893.

Mr. Ewing is the son of William Ewing, of Manor Hill, Huntingdon County, Pennsylvania.

2 MARGARET McCORD.[5]

2 MARGARET McCORD[5] was born April 14, 1856, and was married by Rev. J. M. Adair to JOHN T. POWELL, December 6, 1883. Mr. Powell was born July 28, 1858. His parents were Joseph and Rachael Powell of Stone Valley, Huntingdon County, Pennsylvania. They moved West in March, 1884. They farm and own their own farm near Green Center, Green County, Iowa. They have three children, all living.

JOSEPH M. POWELL,[6] born September 7, 1886.

ALTA JANET POWELL,[6] born July 14, 1888.

LAURA ALICE POWELL,[6] born July 29, 1895.

At present they are attending the M. E. Church, but intend to sell out and move to Keota, Iowa, so as to be near their own church, the United Presbyterian.

Mrs. Samuel McCord died October 30, 1882, aged sixty years. Mr. Samuel McCord died May 9, 1886, aged sixty-nine years.

7 HETTY BARR.[4]

7 HETTY BARR[4] and her brother ROBERT were twins, born on the East Branch, Huntingdon County, Pennsylvania, April 5, 1825. She is the only one of the family living. She still lives three miles from McAlevy's Fort, near where she was born.

She married SAMUEL PORTER October 16, 1849. He died September 12, 1858. He was a farmer. There were born to them two sons and two daughters.

JOHN PORTER[5] was born on July 17, 1850. He is unmarried and makes a home for his aged mother on the farm.

MARY ANNA PORTER[5] was born September 23, 1853, is unmarried and makes her home with her mother.

WILLIAM HOWARD PORTER,[5] born August 15, 1855, died September 22, 1873.

JEANETTE BORLAND PORTER,[5] born September 15, 1858, was married to ALEX CLAY HAGENS March 18, 1893. They lived in Stone Valley. He was a farmer. She died after many months of suffering, on September 9, 1900. She had no children.

8 ROBERT BARR.[4]

8 ROBERT BARR,[4] the twin of HETTY BARR, was born April 5, 1825, on the East Branch, Stone Valley, Huntingdon County, Pennsylvania. He married NANCY PORTER May 1, 1849, and lived at Boalsburg, Centre County, Pennsylvania. He died April 26, 1900, from the effects of la grippe. He was a member of the Presbyterian Church. He followed farming. There were born to them three sons and two daughters.

CYRUS BARR[5] lives at Gatesburg.

HOWARD BARR[5] lives at Gatesburg.

HETTIE GATES BARR[5] lives at Gatesburg.

EMALINE BARR[5] lives at Bellefonte.

HOMER BARR[5] lives at Boalsburg.

IV JAMES BARR.[3]

4 JAMES BARR,[3] fourth son of ROBERT BARR,[2] was born in Kishacoquillas Valley, Mifflin County, Pennsylvania. But little is known of him. He went to Ohio when a young man, and then to Iowa, and died there. Nothing further is known of him.

V ROBERT BARR.[3]

5 ROBERT BARR,[3] the fifth son of ROBERT BARR,[2] was probably born in Kishocaquillas Valley. He afterward moved to Stone Valley. He married his cousin, ELIZABETH BARR,[3] a daughter of DAVID BARR.[2] She died young and left two sons and a daughter.

Mr. Barr died a short time after. His death was peculiarly sad. It was a very customary thing in those days for men to frequent the distillery, which was near the fort, although they were not known often to get drunk. He was out one very cold night, and going by the distillery he stopped to get a little liquor to warm him up. He was found the next morning frozen to death. His little dog, which always followed him, went home and gave the alarm, acting so strangely that they followed him. He led them to the body of his master. The dog was kept with great care in the family until he died of old age. Mr. Barr so far as we can learn was not addicted specially to the use of strong drink, and for this reason was more easily effected.

There were three children.

The daughter's name was Christian. She died young of fever.

The sons were—

1 DAVID BARR.[4]

2 REED BARR.[4]

1 DAVID BARR.[4]

1 DAVID BARR[4] was born October 6, 1813. He was married to ISABELLE COLE December 27, 1855. She was born September 13, 1823. They belonged to the Presbyterian Church of Pine Grove Mills, Center County, Pennsylvania, near to where they lived. Mr. Barr being left motherless was raised (so the friends tell us) by his Aunt Polly, who married a man by the name of McCORMICK, who lived and died at Boalsburg, Center

County, Pennsylvania. David Barr and his brother Reed both married and lived on small farms at the foot of Tussy Mountains, one mile east of Pine Grove Mills, Center County, Pennsylvania. They bought the land together September 1, 1854, and then divided it equally afterward.

David Barr learned chair-making when a young man, at Boalsburg. He afterward learned the painting business. He and his brother Reed worked together. They painted the United Presbyterian Church near McAlevy's Fort, also my father's barn and house, about forty years ago. It lasted so well, they have not been painted since.

Mr. David Barr died of Bright's disease September 24, 1884, and his wife died September 16, 1898, of consumption. Both are buried at Pine Grove Mills cemetery.

They had four children, two sons and two daughters.

1 ROBERT REED BARR[5] was born November 26, 1856. He is a blacksmith by trade and unmarried. He is at present at Ironton, Colorado.

2 BARBARA ALICE BARR[5] was born July 5, 1859, and married Mr. J. B. PIPER April 12, 1887. They live at Pine Grove Mills, Pennsylvania, and have two children.

BELL FLORENCE PIPER,[6] born June 10, 1888.

ANNA MARGARET PIPER,[6] born April 26, 1899.

Mr. Piper belongs to the German Reformed and Mrs. Piper to the Presbyterian Church. Mr. Piper is a coachmaker by trade.

3 ANNA ELIZABETH BARR[5] was born June 15, 1861. She is a seamstress in Pine Grove Mills Pennsylvania. She is a member of the Presbyterian Church.

4 WILLIAM ARMSTRONG BARR[5] was born February 11, 1865. and died January 31, 1887. He was a teacher.

The family are all in the church and interested in the work of the Lord.

2 REED BARR.[4]

2 REED BARR[4] was born July 9, 1815. He was raised by his Aunt Polly McCormick until he was nine years of age, and then he was put out for his board and clothes.

Reed Barr was a small man and somewhat delicate, but a jovial, kindly dispositioned man. He and his brother David were orphans together, worked together, and lived neighbors all their lives.

Mr. Reed Barr had a great many cherry trees on his place, and the young folks of us often drove over the mountain at the close of wheat harvest for cherries, and always enjoyed a good time.

Mr. Reed Barr when a young man taught school in the winter season. He taught near our home one winter at what was known as Steffie's schoolhouse, in Stone Valley, Pennsylvania.

He was married to MARY WILLIAMSON, of Stone Valley, October 1, 1850, by Rev. William Hamill, of Oak Hall, Center County, Pennsylvania. Reed Barr died May 17, 1891, aged seventy-five years and ten months. He died at his home and was buried at Pine Grove Mills, Pennsylvania. His children still own the homestead. David and Sallie Barr still live there.

Mrs. Reed Barr was a daughter of Hugh and Mary Williamson, and was born in Jefferson County, Pennsylvania, May 3, 1822, and died April 7, 1886, aged sixty-three years, eleven months and four days. She died at her home in Center County, and was buried alongside of her husband. She came from Jefferson County to Huntingdon County when she was sixteen years old.

The children born to them are as follows:

1 HUGH WILLIAMSON BARR.[5]
2 MARY ELIZABETH BARR.[5]

Mr. John S. Barr.

(Page 60.)

3 SARAH JANE BARR.[5]
4 DAVID BARR.[5]
5 ROBERT ELMER BARR.[5]

1 HUGH WILLIAM BARR.[5]

1 HUGH W. BARR[5] was born at Boalsburg, September 29, 1851. He is still living at Salina, Kansas, where he moved March 5, 1878. He married ALICE E. LOPSHIRE (born at Fort Wayne, Indiana, November 1, 1864) at Salina, Kansas, February 26, 1882. Their children were all born in Salina County, Kansas.

Infant son, born January 28, 1883, died February 5, 1883.

NORA MAY BARR,[6] born March 14, 1885.

ELMER BARR[6], ELSIE BARR[6], } born July 11, 1887. (They were twins.)

MARY ELIZABETH BARR,[6] born March 31, 1889.

RAY REED BARR,[6] born March 9, 1894, died December 7, 1895. Died of membranous croup.

BERTHA ALICE BARR,[6] born February 19, 1897.

Mr. Barr is a laborer.

2 MARY ELIZABETH BARR.[5]

2 MARY E. BARR[5] was born April 15, 1856, and died December 1, 1892, aged thirty six years, seven months and sixteen days. She married GEORGE W. GATES December 20, 1887. They moved to the farm of Mr. Sterrett Cummins, two miles east of McAlevy's Fort, Huntingdon County, in the spring of 1889. They remained there two years, and from there moved to John A. Wilson's farm, one-half mile west of McAlevy's Fort (the farm owned by my father, James Barr), and Mrs. Gates died there and was buried with her people at Pine Grove Mills. They had no children.

3 SARAH JANE BARR.[5]

3 SARAH J. BARR was born March 27, 1858. She is single and lives with her brother David on the homestead.

4 DAVID BARR.[5]

4 DAVID BARR[5] was born January 28, 1860, and lives on the homestead.   David has been treasurer of the Sunday-school of the Presbyterian Church at Pine Grove Mills for six years, and was superintendent for five years.

5 ROBERT ELMER BARR.[5]

5 ROBERT E. BARR[5] was born February 5, 1863.   He lives at Camp Bird, Ouray County, Colorado.   He cooks in a boarding-house.   He started West on May 8, 1893, first going to North Dakota for three months, then to the state of Washington for a short time.   From there he went to California, then to Arizona for three years, and from there he went to Colorado, where he is at present.   He has been cooking ever since he went West.

The parents and children of both families were all piously inclined, and early joined the Presbyterian Church.

They started poor in life, but have been able to make a respectable living and enjoy a good measure of comfort, and all bear a good name and have the confidence and respect of the community in which they live.

VI ELIZABETH BARR.[3]

6 ELIZABETH BARR,[3] the eldest daughter of ROBERT[2] and CHRISTIAN (REED) BARR, was born in Kishacoquillas Valley, Mifflin County, Pennsylvania.   The date of her birth we cannot obtain.   She never married.   She made a home for Reed and David Barr after they were nine years old, and their father, Robert Barr, had died.   She lived at Boalsburg, Center Coun-

ty, Pennsylvania. After Reed and David were married and moved to their own places near Pine Grove Mills, in the same county, she made her home with Reed Barr until her death, March 8, 1856, and was buried at Pine Grove Mills cemetery. She occupied an important place, and seemed to be raised up for a special mission; and she must have filled it well, for both the boys grew up to be good, religious men, and raised respectable families.

VII MARY BARR.[3]

7 MARY BARR[3] was born in Kishacoquillas Valley, Mifflin County, Pennsylvania. We do not have the date of her birth. She married HUGH WILLIAMSON, and moved to Jefferson County, Pennsylvania. They were probably married about 1820. They had two children.

   1 ROBERT WILLIAMSON [4]
   2 MARY WILLIAMSON.[4]

Mr. Williamson's wife died, and he married again and had four children. Mr. Williamson and both wives died in Jefferson County, Pennsylvania.

1 ROBERT WILLIAMSON.[4]

1 ROBERT WILLIAMSON[4] married MARGARET McALEVY, daughter of Allen and Letitia McAlevy, who lived in Iowa. They were married in 1846. He made his home in Stone Valley, Huntingdon County, Pennsylvania. He and his family were members of the United Presbyterian Church, and very regular in their attendance upon the services of the church. Mr. Williamson died of pneumonia, in Stone Valley, Pennsylvania, where they made their home, in 1897. Mrs. Williamson died the following year, 1898. They had ten children.

MARY,[5] who makes her home with Rev. J. M. Adair, New
Sheffield, Pennsylvania. She has lived in his home
since 1881. She is a faithful, good girl and is filling an
important place.

HUGH WILLIAMSON.[5]

JAMES WILLIAMSON.[5]

LETITIA WILLIAMSON.[5]

REED WILLIAMSON.[5]

RUTH WILLIAMSON.[5]

SAMUEL WILLIAMSON.[5]

JOHN WILLIAMSON.[5]

ELIZABETH WILLIAMSON.[5]

NANNIE WILLIAMSON.[5]

Most of the children are living in Stone Valley. A complete record of the family could not be obtained.

2 MARY WILLIAMSON.[4]

2 MARY WILLIAMSON,[4] daughter of HUGH and MARY WIL-
LIAMSON, was born May 3, 1822, probably in Jefferson County,
Pennsylvania. She was married to REED BARR (her full cousin), of Boalsburg, Center County, Pennsylvania, October 1, 1850,
by Rev. Wm. Hamill, of Oak Hall, Center County, Pennsylvania. (See REED BARR, page 50.)

This closes the first family record, which takes in 295
names, not counting the unnamed infants, which would make
over 300 persons born into the family.

This is rather remarkable in point of numbers, and also
just as remarkable in point of character. There would be little
use for a constabulary, if the world was made up of such families.
Their record is a clean one throughout, and their standing
honorable, wherever they lived. The God of Jacob has been
their God, and Jacob's blessing upon *his* sons, has rested upon
them. It pays to be loyal to God and his truth.

FAMILY II.

DAVID BARR.[2]

DAVID BARR,[2] second son of ROBERT[1] and MARY WILLS BARR, was born in Ireland in 1750, and came to this country some years in advance of the rest of the family, accompanied by his older brother Robert. He was married in this country to Miss SARAH THOMPSON, of Carlisle, Cumberland County, Pennsylyania. He first settled in Kishacoquillas Valley, Mifflin County, Pennsylvania. The country was very new at that time, and wild game, wildcats, bears, wolves, wild turkeys, etc., abounded. And the Indians also were plentiful.

Grandfather in his memoirs says that on October 22 and 23, 1790 (about the time they arrived at Lewistown, or Oldtown), "Brigadier-General Harmer, with about 300 men under his command, had an engagement with the hostile Indians at the Miami villages. He lost about 183 men. However, he kept his ground and burned the Indian villages and the Maumee towns, and took a vast store of corn and forage."

This reads to us in our day like ancient history. They had forts built of stone in various localities, where the natives could gather to defend themselves when the Indians put on the war paint and got troublesome. One such fort was built a half mile from the writer's home, in Huntingdon County, Pennsylvania, called "McAlevy's Fort," after old General McAlevy, one of the earliest settlers.

David Barr is reported by some of the friends to have been in the Revolutionary War, but in looking over the army lists of Pennsylvania, we could not verify it. He was a farmer, and with his son was engaged at threshing wheat when his brothers from Ireland—who had just arrived—called upon him. He did not know them, and they did not make themselves known to him (like Joseph of Bible times) for some little time, and when they did tell him he was greatly surprised and wonderfully pleased. This shows that he and his brother Robert had been in this country for some years, perhaps before the Revolutionary War, as they did not know their own brothers, who were men about thirty-three years of age at that time.

The earliest mention of his name is in a call for a pastor extended to Rev. James Johnston, dated March 15, 1783. It commences, "We the subscribers, members of the United Congregation of East and West Kishacoquillas," etc., and is signed by fifty or seventy-five persons. David Barr was an elder in the Presbyterian Church at that time. This was found in Mifflin County history. Also in the same history we find the assessment for Armagh township, Mifflin County, in 1790, and among the taxpayers mentioned therein is David Barr as possessed of 200 acres of land, two horses and two cows; also his brother Robert Barr assessed for two horses and two cows.

He must have moved soon after this to Center County, for in the Center County history we find the following references to David Barr: In the organization of the county in 1800 the first county commissioners were David Barr and two others. Also that the first grand jury in this county assembled in April, 1801, and David Barr was one of the jurymen. Associated with him on the grand jury were the names of General Bennen, William Irvine and General Patton. These were probably generals who took part in the Revolutionary War.

Mr. David Barr lived within two miles of Boalsburg, Center County, Pennsylvania, and both he and his wife died and were buried there. Mr. Barr died at the age of eighty-five, in the year 1835.

They reared a large, intelligent, and very respectable family, consisting of nine childen—five sons and four daughters.

I ROBERT BARR.[3]
II DAVID BARR.[3]
III WILLIAM WILLS BARR.[3]
IV SAMUEL BARR.[3]
V JOHN BARR.[3]
VI POLLY BARR.[3]
VII JENNIE BARR.[3]
VIII MARGARET BARR.[3]
IX MARY BARR.[3]

As we do not have the ages of the members of David Barr's[2] family, we are unable to say in what order they come. All we know is that Robert was the oldest, and we have learned as we were going to press that William Wills (marked third) was the youngest of the family. If anything should be learned later it will be found in the Supplement.

I ROBERT BARR.[3]

1 ROBERT BARR[3] was born in 1775, and married ELIZABETH BRISBIN in 1800. He moved with his parents to Center County, Pennsylvania, when a boy. He lived in Center County for twenty-five years after his marriage. All his family were born in this county. He moved to Corsica, Clarion County, Pennsylvania, in 1825, and died there June 1, 1848. His wife died in 1845. He was a Democrat in politics, and a tanner by trade. There were born to them eight children.

1 NANCY BARR.[4]
2 DAVID BARR.[4]
3 THOMPSON BARR.[4]
4 SARAH BARR.[4]
5 ROBERT BARR.[4]
6 ELIZABETH BARR.[4]
7 SAMUEL BARR.[4]
8 WILLIAM BARR.[4]

1 NANCY BARR.[4]

1 NANCY BARR[4] married HENRY DULL and lived in western[4] Pennsylvania. She died January 28, 1841. They have one son.

HENRY DULL[5] lives at Brockwayville, Jefferson County, Pennsylvania. He is engaged in the lumber business. We know nothing of the rest of the family.

2 DAVID BARR.[4]

2 DAVID BARR[4] died in 1835.

3 THOMPSON BARR.[4]

3 THOMPSON BARR[4] died in April, 1858, of consumption. He was sheriff of Clarion County, and died in Brookville. He never married.

4 SARAH BARR.[4]

4 SARAH BARR[4] never married. She died January 28, 1841.

5 ROBERT BARR.[4]

5 ROBERT BARR[4] was born in 1811 and lived near Corsica, Clarion County. He died in 1892, at the age of eighty-one years. He was a farmer.

6 ELIZABETH BARR.[4]

6 ELIZABETH BARR[4] was born November 22, 1814. She married JOHNSTON J. CORBETT in 1834. He was born in 1813. They lived happily together for sixty years. They united with the Presbyterian Church the next year after they were married, in 1835. She died February 24, 1894, in her eightieth year. Mr. Corbett is still living at Richardsville, Jefferson County, Pennsylvania, in his eighty-seventh year.

They had eleven children, all of whom are dead but three. Three of their sons were in the Civil War. The children were all members of the Presbyterian Church.

Mr. Samuel W. Barr and Wife.

(Page 65.)

7 SAMUEL BARR.[4]

7 SAMUEL BARR[4] died in Tennessee in 1875.

8 WILLIAM BARR.[4]

8 WILLIAM BARR[4] died in the army during the Civil War, in 1862.

They were all Democrats except the oldest and youngest sons. The history of this family is very meager. It was with difficulty that we secured even this much.

II DAVID BARR.[3]

2 DAVID BARR[3] was born in Center County, Pennsylvania, near Boalsburg, in 1794, and moved to Jefferson County in 1830, when he was thirty-six years of age. He married RACHAEL PAXTON, daughter of Colonel Paxton of Revolutionary fame.

Mr. Barr was in the war of 1812. The family records were lost and we cannot get exact dates. His wife was born in 1794. She died in 1854, at the age of sixty. Mr Barr died in 1856, at the age of sixty-two. They both died on the farm to which they moved, near Clarion, Pennsylvania. There were born to them three sons and five daughters.

    1 JOSEPH BARR.[4]
    2 MAHALA ANN BARR.[4]
    3 ELIZABETH BARR.[4]
    4 MARGARET BARR.[4]
    5 JOHN S. BARR.[4]
    6 SAMUEL PAXTON BARR.[4]
    7 DAVID BARR.[4]
    8 RACHAEL BARR.[4]

1 JOSEPH BARR.[4]

1 JOSEPH BARR,[4] born in 1815, died in infancy.

2 MAHALA ANN BARR.[4]

2 MAHALA ANN BARR[4] was born near Boalsburg May 26, 1818. She was married to WASHINGTON TAYLOR March 13, 1834, and died in 1848. She left one son, DAVID JACKSON TAYLOR, who lives in the State of Washington.

3 ELIZABETH BARR.[4]

3 ELIZABETH BARR[4] was born near Boalsburg, Pennsylvania, February 20, 1820. She is eighty years of age and still living at Oil City, Pennsylvania. She married a Mr. BORLAND.

4 MARGARET BARR.[4]

4 MARGARET BARR[4] was born March 20, 1821, near Boalsburg. She also married a Mr. BORLAND, cousin of her sister's husband.

5 JOHN S. BARR.[4]

5 JOHN S. BARR[4] was born May 26, 1825, near Boalsburg, Pennsylvania. He married NANCY J. ANTHONY. Mr. Barr was elected sheriff of Jefferson County in 1872. He was elected in 1893 as Register Recorder and Clerk of the Orphans' Court, and in 1896 was re-elected to the same office by a majority of 2200, which showed his popularity. His son-in-law, John D. Evans, was elected last fall (1899) to the same office.

He started in the hotel business in Pittsburg and has since had charge of the American hotel in Brookville, Jefferson County, Pennsylvania, where he still lives. He and his family are active members of the Presbyterian Church. He has been suffering with cancer of the right hand for eighteen months, and can scarcely write. We are much indebted to Mr. Barr for the record of the families in western Pennsylvania. He has been burned out twice, and lost all his family records, so that many of the dates cannot be given. To them were born six children.

1 AGNES S. BARR[5] was born February 19, 1851. She married ROBERT KELLY October 25, 1866. They live near Brookville, Pennsylvania. To them were born six children, as follows :

MAME SMYERS KELLY,[6] born May 12, 1870.

JOHN T. KELLY,[6] born April 11, 1874.

WILLIAM E. KELLY,[6] born January 21, 1877.

LOTTIE E. KELLY,[6] born May 11, 1879.

EARL C. KELLY,[6] born November 16, 1881.

GEORGE H. KELLY,[6] born August 1, 1885.

2 MARY ELIZABETH BARR[5] was born January 4, 1862. She was married to JOSEPH McDONALD, and lives near Brookville. Their children are as follows:

BERTHA McDONALD,[6] born September 9, 1881. She was married to D. B. HINES.

DAISY McDONALD,[6] born August 6, 1883.

JOSEPH McDONALD,[6] born March 6, 1889.

3 SAMUEL PAXTON BARR[5] was born December 16, 1863. He married MARY DRUMMOND and lives near Brookville, Pennsylvania. To them were born five children.

RUTH BARR,[6] born August 31, 1889.

JOHN BARR,[6] born March 1, 1891.

MYRTLE BARR,[6] born November 13, 1892.

NANCY BARR,[6] born in 1895.

MARTHA BARR,[6] born June 14, 1899.

4 JOHN W. BARR,[5] born August 7, 1866. He married BELL MOGLE. They live in Punxsutawney, Pennsylvania.

5 GEORGE M. BARR[5] was born June 17, 1868. He married LIZZIE FITZGERALD. They have two children. They live near Brookville, Pennsylvania.

GERALD BARR,[6] born in March, 1894.

BLANCH BARR,[6] born in October, 1896.

6 BLANCH C. BARR[5] was married to JOHN D. EVANS in 1889. She was born February 22, 1873. Mr. Evans was born in 1866. They live in Brookville, Pennsylvania. He was elected Register Recorder and Clerk of the Orphans' Court of the county of Jefferson, Pennsylvania, November, 1899. They have three children.

HELEN M. EVANS,[6] born March 3, 1890.

BESSIE B. EVANS,[6] born August 17, 1891.

MARY J. EVANS,[6] born February 14, 1895.

6 SAMUEL PAXTON BARR.[4]

6 SAMUEL PAXTON BARR[4] was born 1815. In his younger days he preached in the Baptist Church. He was engaged in the mercantile business for fifteen years, and was also justice of the peace. He died in 1887, aged seventy-two years.

7 DAVID BARR.[4]

7 DAVID BARR[4] died in 1851, when a young man.

8 RACHAEL BARR.[4]

8 RACHAEL BARR[4] was born August 10, 1828, near Boalsburg, Pennsylvania. She has been married twice. Her first marriage was to JOHN PORTER, in Butler County, Pennsylvania. To this union two children were born.

1 SAMUEL THOMPSON PORTER[5] was born February 14, 1848. He was married to AMANDA R. LITTLE, daughter of Abram O. and Eveline Ellenor (Reynolds) Little, December 23, 1875. She was born in Meadville, Pennsylvania, February 26, 1857. Mr. Porter and family moved to Kansas in November, 1878. His occupation is stone-masonry and plastering. Their children are—

EVA MAY PORTER,[6] born in Meadville, Pennsylvania, October 12, 1876.

MABEL D. PORTER,[6] born in Graham County, Kansas, August 6, 1880.

RACHAEL PORTER,[6] born in Logan, Phillips County, Kansas, November 22, 1882.

JULIA CLAIR PORTER,[6] born in Logan, Phillips County, Kansas, June 14, 1889.

EVA MAY PORTER[6] married HENRY W. NORRISH, M. D., August 18, 1897. Dr. Norrish was born in London, England, February 10, 1870. He came to America in 1872. He graduated from Ensworth Medical College, St. Joseph, Missouri, in 1894, and Missouri Medical College, St. Louis, Missouri, in 1895. They have one child.

> ELLEN MAE NORRISH,[7] born in Logan, Phillips County, Kansas, May 16, 1898.

2 JULIA PORTER,[5] daughter of John and Rachael Porter,[4] was born December 30, 1850. She lives at 1614 Winfield Street, Los Angeles, California, with her half-sister, Mrs. Pardee.

Mrs. Rachael Porter's[4] second marriage, was to NATHANIEL M. WASSON, who was born November 23, 1823. He served in the Civil War, enlisting in the Sixteenth Pennsylvania Cavalry, but was not in any battle. Mr. Wasson's father was in the war of 1812, under General Harrison. Mr. and Mrs. Wasson live near Meadville, Pennsylvania, Pettis Road, Rural Route No. 3. To this union were born seven children.

1 DAVID S WASSON[5] was born in Butler County, Pennsylvania, December 11, 1856, and lives at present in Bristol, Harrison County, West Virginia. He married MISS ANNIE BURFORD, daughter of David Burford, of Venango County, Pennsylvania. They have three children.

MABLE WASSON,[6] who was born in Crawford County, Pennsylvania, May 27, 1878. She married Mr. KREAPS and resides in Parkersburg, West Virginia. They have one child.

LOWRIE KREAPS,[7] born May 27, 1898.

LILLIAN WASSON,[6] born in McKean County, Pennsylvania, June 2, 1880, married Mr. KISER and lives in Crawford County, Pennsylvania.

OWEN M. WASSON,[6] born in Butler County, Pennsylvania, May 6, 1885.

2 JOHN M. WASSON[5] was born July 16, 1859. He lives in Fostoria, Seneca County, Ohio, Rural Route No. 2.

3 EMMA WASSON,[5] born December 15, 1861, died August 17, 1864.

4 E. D. WASSON,[5] born in March, 1864, was married to EVA V. CAMPBELL, youngest daughter of Robert and Nancy Campbell, at Fairview, Butler County, Pennsylvania, May 5, 1885. She was born September 23, 1866, three miles from Murrinsville, Butler County, Pennsylvania. They live at Tionesta, Forest County, Pennsylvania. Mr. Wasson's business is contracting and drilling oil wells. He has been in the oil business since 1882. They have four children.

LERY WASSON,[6] born August 1, 1886.

MYRTLE M. WASSON,[6] born February 15, 1888.

LUCY G. WASSON,[6] born October 7, 1892.

ROBERT M. WASSON,[6] born March 28, 1897.

5 LUCY E. WASSON,[5] born October 7, 1866, is married to Mr. PARDEE, and lives at 1614 Winfield Street, Los Angeles, California.

6 EVA WASSON,[5] born May 3, 1869, died September 17, 1870.

7 CHARLES H. WASSON,[5] born April 26, 1875, lives at Findlay, Ohio.

III WILLIAM WILLS BARR.[3]

3 WILLIAM W. BARR[3] was born July 19, 1794, in Mifflin County, Pennsylvania. He married JANE SEMPLE in 1813. He died of a rupture when he was forty-two years and eleven months old, on June 19, 1837. Jane Semple Barr was born July 5, 1792, and died September 9, 1850, aged fifty-eight years and two months. They both died at the Barr homestead, near Boalsburg, Center County, Pennsylvania. There were born to them seven sons and three daughters.

    1 SAMUEL W. BARR.[4]
    2 DAVID BARR.[4]
    3 JANE A. BARR.[4]
    4 JAMES S. BARR.[4]
    5 THOMPSON BARR.[4]
    6 HON. WILLIAM WILLS BARR.[4]
    7 ALEXANDER B. BARR.[4]
    8 GEORGE BARR.[4]
    9 SALLIE BARR.[4]
  10 ASENATH BARR.[4]

1 SAMUEL W. BARR.[4]

1 SAMUEL W. BARR[4] was born May 9, 1814. He married SARAH L. MENOLD, in Mercer County, Pennsylvania, June 23, 1845. They moved west in 1857. He first lived in Ohio, and then moved to Illinois. He died at Aledo, Illinois, October 8, 1898, in his eighty-fifth year.

He was in his usual health and went to the well to draw some water, and as he was returning fell dead on the door-step without making a sound.

He was born in Center County, Pennsylvania, two miles from Boalsburg. All the brothers and sisters were born at the same place. He was a member of the United Presbyterian

Church of Aledo. He had a large family, eleven children having been born to them.

1 LIZZIE BARR,[5] born January, 1851, died November, 1868.

2 HELEN BARR,[5] born August 23, 1852, died September, 1854.

3 WILLIAM H. BARR[5] was born March 3, 1854. He married MAGGIE MURTLAND, daughter of Alex and Fannie Murtland, at Fountain Greene, Illinois, March 3, 1880. She was born October 8, 1856. They live in Aledo, Illinois. His business is burning brick. They have nine children.

> CHARLES BLAIR BARR,[6] born December 13, 1880.
> ALSON J. STEETER BARR,[6] born September 5, 1882.
> ETHYL BARR,[6] born May 3, 1884.
> CLARENCE COLE BARR,[6] born March 18, 1886.
> MABEL CLAIR BARR,[6] born November 18, 1887.
> HARRY ANDREW BARR,[6] born August 18, 1889.
> FANNIE MURTLAND BARR,[6] born March 29, 1891.
> LYLIS VERL BARR,[6] born April 6, 1893.
> JOE BOHR BARR,[6] born October 29, 1895.

4 ANDREW C. BARR[5] was born in Center County, Pennsylvania, February 14, 1856. He married MARY A. TARY, the eldest daughter of John and Sarah Ann Tary, May 30, 1892. She was born January 26, 1863. They live near Viola, Illinois. He is a coal miner. They have two sons.

> GEORGE I. BARR,[6] born November 26, 1892.
> REUBEN MILES BARR,[6] born December 29, 1897.

5 IDA BARR[5] was born August 26, 1859, in Illinois. She married MONT GEDDES. He is a farmer and lives near Aledo, Illinois. They have one daughter, LILLIE GEDDES.

Mrs. Jane A. Barr.

(Page 67.)

6 ALBERT BARR[5] was born February 4, 1862, in Illinois. He married MARIA STEPHENS. They live near Ottumwa, Iowa. He is a farmer. They have had two boys. One of them died.

7 LAURA BARR[5] was born in Mercer County, Illinois, August 26, 1864. She married JOSEPH F. McDOUGAL in Iowa City, Iowa, February 10, 1892. He was born in Mercer County, Illinois, in 1860. He is a traveling man. They live in Aledo, Illinois. They have one daughter.

GLADYS FERN McDOUGAL,[6] born June 22, 1897.

8 CARRIE BARR[5] was born March 4, 1867. She married HENRY JOBUSCH, son of Lewis F. and Ann K. Jobusch, December 24, 1885. They live at Aledo, Illinois. He follows horse training for a business. They have three children.

MARY JOBUSCH,[6] born December 12, 1886.

ROSE JOBUSCH,[6] born June 23, 1888.

FREDDIE JOBUSCH,[6] born October 26, 1892.

9 FELTON BARR,[5] born August 21, 1869, died February, 1884.

10 SALLIE W. BARR,[5] born May 26, 1872, died January 19, 1881.

11 ROSE BARR,[5] born April 26, 1858, died November, 1858.

2 DAVID BARR.[4]

2 DAVID BARR[4] was born in 1818, and died when a young man, December 19, 1834. He was buried the very day his sister Sallie was born.

3 JANE A. BARR.[4]

3 JANE A. BARR[4] was born in Center County, near Boalsburg, Pennsylvania, July 27, 1820. She was married to

DAVID BARR, her second cousin, and son of Samuel and Lydia (Block) Barr, September 26, 1844, by Rev. Mr. Adams. They moved West in the fall of 1860 to West Point, Iowa; and then again in 1862 to Big Mound, Iowa, and in 1864 to Fountain Greene, Hancock County, Illinois, where they lived until recently. The daughters having all married and gone to them selves but Nannie, they moved to Carthage, Illinois, where they live together. (See record of DAVID BARR,[8] son of Samuel Barr,[2] for further account.)

4 JAMES S. BARR, Sr.[4]

4 JAMES S. BARR[4] was born in Center County, Pennsyl-vania, near Boalsburg, November 26, 1822. He was married to CHARLOTTE B. STAGE. She was born February 20, 1817, and died March 20, 1897, from the effects of a severe cold. Mr. Barr died of cancer, May 29, 1899, at Boskydell, Jackson County, Illinois, where he lived on a farm.

They came east to Indiana in 1857, and the following year moved to Tamaroa, Perry County, Illinois. Some time after that he moved to Benton, Franklin County, Illinois, and lastly to Carbondale, Jackson County, Illinois.

For ten years before going west he was editor of the *Huntingdon American*, Huntingdon County, Pennsylvania. After moving west he edited and published the *American Spy* in Perry County, Illinois. In 1863 he published the *Benton Standard* (a Democratic paper), in Jackson County, Illinois, and continued in that capacity until 1878, when he retired to a farm near Carbondale, where he died.

During his residence at Benton he served as county clerk and master in chancery for several terms. In Pennsylvania he was prominent in educational circles, and served his native county several terms as superintendent of schools. In southern Illinois, he was recognized as a vigorous writer upon all public

questions, and during his years of active service no writer was
more generally quoted in that section. After retiring from the
newspaper work, he devoted himself to his farm, in which he
took great pride, and which might be called a model fruit farm.

They were consistent members of the Presbyterian Church.
His wife joined the church in 1855. All her children—seven
in number—survive her. She left a large circle of friends,
who mourn her loss, but who have the satisfaction of knowing
that she has entered upon a reward justly earned by a life of
unselfish devotion to her husband and children, and the exercise
of a Christian fortitude that never faltered or grew weary.
Her's was a beautiful life, filled with good deeds, and behind
her she left an example worthy of emulation by all.

Their children consisted of five daughters and two sons.

1 WILLIAM WILLS BARR.[5]

2 MAGGIE BARR.[5]

3 CHARLOTTE BARR.[5]

4 JAMES S. BARR.[5]

5 CLARA S. BARR.[5]

6 EMMA BARR.[5]

7 FLORA BARR.[5]

1 HON. WILLIAM WILLS BARR.[5]

1 HON. WILLIAM WILLS BARR[6] was born in Center County,
Pennsylvania, May 8, 1845. He married ALICE GLEIN BREN-
IZEN, daughter of Joseph Addison and Christina Glein Brenizen,
at Philadelphia, Pennsylvania, January 15, 1850.

He is a prominent attorney and lives in Carbondale, Jackson County, Illinois. He was a member of the Illinois House of
Repesentatives from 1870 to 1872; Master in Chancery of Franklin County, Illinois, two terms; State's attorney of same county
for four years, from 1872 to 1876; Judge of County Court of
Jackson County, Illinois, for eight years, serving two terms,

commencing in 1887. He was Grand Orator for the Grand Lodge of Illinois A. F. and A. M., and Grand Spectator of the Knights of Honor of the State of Illinois for two years. He is at present attorney for the Illinois Central Railroad Company, and several other corporations. Judge Barr in politics is a Democrat.

There were born to this union two daughters.

JESSIE GLEIN BARR,[6] born in 1875, married DR. ROBERT E. STEEL, of Sehi City, Utah.

BERTHA ALICE BARR,[6] born in 1877, married DR. W. H. KUSEE, of Carbondale, Illinois, May 25, 1895.

2 MAGGIE BARR.[5]

2 MAGGIE BARR[5] was born in Huntingdon, Pennsylvania, May 26, 1858. She married DR. A. G. ORR, son of William H. and Charlotte (Penny) Orr, of Wilson County, Tennessee, in 1879. His maternal grandfather (James Penny) was a resident of the State of North Carolina, while his grandfather on his father's side was a Kentuckian, who served under General Harrison at the battle of Tippecanoe.

Dr. Orr was born September 19, 1841. He was educated in the higher branches at the Cumberland University, but during the Civil War joined the Confederate army as a member of the heavy artillery service, and served until the conclusion of hostilities, when he returned to pursue the study of medicine. He graduated from the Jefferson Medical College of Philadelphia, in 1867. In the same year he located at Benton, Illinois, for the practice of his profession. There he has labored faithfully and ably, and prospered accordingly. He is among the oldest and most substantial practitioners of Franklin County, Illinois. He is a member of the Southern Illinois Medical Association, and a local surgeon of the C. & E. I. Railroad Company. He is identified with the Free Masons, Knights of Honor, and Golden Cross orders.

Hon. William W. Barr.

(Page 69.)

To them were born six children, who are all living.

WILLIAM J. ORR,[6] the eldest son, is a graduate of the Benton High School, and a promising young man.

ARTHUR G. ORR,[6] who is married.

EDWARD H. ORR.[6]

LILLIAN ORR.[6]

ROBERT B. ORR.[6]

CHARLES C. ORR.[6]

3 CHARLOTTE BARR.[5]

3 CHARLOTTE BARR[5] married W. L. TABOR. Mr. Tabor is a farmer and lives near Conway, Faulkner County, Arkansas. They have one daughter.

4 JAMES S. BARR.[5]

4 JAMES S. BARR, JR.,[5] is married and lives in Carterville, Illinois. He is editor of a paper, and in politics is a Republican. They have three children, two boys and a girl.

5 CLARA J. BARR.[5]

5 CLARA J. BARR[5] makes her home with her brother, Judge W. W. Barr, of Carbondale, Illinois. She is unmarried.

6 EMMA BARR.[5]

6 EMMA BARR[5] married Mr. FRED WEBB, of Kansas City, Missouri. He is a cattle buyer and shipper. They live at Kansas, City. Mr. Webb is a Democrat. They have one son, RALPH BARR.[6]

7 FLORA BARR.[5]

7 FLORA BARR[5] was born in Huntingdon, Pennsylvania, May 26, 1858. She was married to JOHN A. Ross October 5, 1879, at Dover, Pope County, Arkansas, by Rev. J. L. Hicks. Mr. Ross was born in Gibson County, Tennessee, July 7, 1848. He is a merchant. They have two children.

ETHEL ZENAS ROSS,[6] born in Dardanelle, Arkansas, June 22, 1881.

ALLAN BARR ROSS,[6] born in Dardanelle, Arkansas, April 1, 1891. He is a bright boy in the fourth grade. He is considered one of the best pupils at school, and is always at the head of his class.

We are indebted to Ethel Z. Ross for much of this data.

5 THOMPSON BARR.[4]

5 THOMPSON BARR[4] was born in Penns Valley, Center County, Pennsylvania, in 1825. He married Miss ELLEN SPARR of near Boalsburg, Center County. His first child, Maggie E., was born in Center County. He then moved to Keokuk, Iowa, and while in Iowa there were born to them Jennie, and John S. the only son; afterward Iowa A., the youngest daughter, was born.

Mr. Barr was a man possessed of remarkable memory, a great reader, exceptionally fond of history, well posted, and was a good conversationalist. He was a man of good judgment and unimpeachable integrity. He took a very active part in politics, and was an earnest advocate of the principles of the Republican party. He was a carpenter by trade, at which he worked for many years, both before and after he went West. On account of his wife's health he sold out in the West some time in 1863 and came East. Mrs. Barr died soon after his return from the West. She had been in delicate health for some years before she died. He went to Clarion County along in sixty-nine or seventy, and with his brother Alex. B. Barr built a hotel and storeroom in Clarion, and engaged in the mercantile business. They did an immense business and were quite successful for some years, up to 1885, when he embarked in the oil business, which resulted in his financial ruin, and from which he never fully recovered. He died on Decoration Day, May 30, 1898, of cholera morbus, at Mahaffey, Pennsylvania, at the home of his daughter, Jennie Cromer.

Mr. Thompson Barr.

(Page 72.)

Their children were—

1 MAGGIE E. BARR[5] never married, and died in February, 1896.

2 JENNIE BARR[5] was born in Keokuk, Iowa, in 1857. After her mother's death she was raised by Alex B. Barr, her uncle, who had no children. She was married to a Mr. CROMER at Brookville, Pennsylvania, February 7, 1883, by Rev. Elder. They live at McGees Mills, Pennsylvania. To them were born seven children.

> ALEXANDER BROWN BARR CROMER,[6] born at Brookville, January 11, 1884, is now attending Bellefonte Academy, Bellefonte, Center County, Pennsylvania.
>
> CATHERINE CROMER[6] was born at Brookville, February 24, 1886.
>
> JOHN BOWEN CROMER[6] was born at Punxsutawney, Pennsylvania, August 2, 1890, and died July 20, 1891.
>
> THOMPSON CROMER[6] was born at Glenhope, Clearfield County, Pennsylvania, September 17, 1892.
>
> RACHEL CROMER[6] was born at Mahaffey, Pennsylvania, August 21, 1896.
>
> The twins, MARY and JENNIE CROMER,[6] were born at Mahaffey, January 23, 1898.

3 JOHN S. BARR[5] was born March 21, 1859. He is single. He is in the employ of the American Steel Sheet Company, at Vandergrift, Pennsylvania, forty miles east of Pittsburg.

4 IOWA A. BARR[5] was born September 10, 1860, in the city of Keokuk, Iowa. She was without a name when they moved from Iowa to Pennsylvania, and they called her Iowa. She was married to WALTER E. BANKS May 4, 1896. He was born in England October 27, 1856, and died March 15, 1897. He was a chemist. They

came to New York city September 1, 1896. Mrs. Banks
and son still reside there. She is a member of the
Presbyterian Church. They had one son.

WILLIAM THOMPSON BANKS,[6] born January 27, 1897,
in New York city.

6 HON. WILLIAM WILLS BARR.[4]

6 HON. WILLIAM WILLS BARR[4]—better known as Judge
Barr—was a very successful lawyer, making his home in Clarion
County, Pennsylvania. He was born February 15, 1827, in
Center County, near Boalsburg.

He died suddenly during a terrible fire in Clarion, that
burned his office and the business part of the city. He personally superintended the removal of his law books and furniture
from his office, and must have been in the act of retiring when
he was overcome, for he was discovered lying on the floor. He
was taken quickly to the Coulter House, where he died in a
few minutes. This was in February, 1900, making him seventy-
three years of age. He was a very large man, weighing two
hundred and fifty pounds; perhaps the largest Barr of the name.

Judge Barr attended the public schools of Boalsburg
until he was fifteen years of age, and then taught for a few
years. After this he attended Dickinson Seminary, at Williamsport, Pennsylvania. In 1850 he became a law student in the
office of Joseph Alexander, Esq., at Lewistown, Pennsylvania,
and two years later was admitted to the bar of that county.
He went to Clarion in 1853 and commenced the practice of
law, and soon built up a lucrative business. He served four
terms as district attorney of that county, and two years as county
treasurer. He was elected a member of the General Assembly
of Pennsylvania from that county in 1864, and again reelected.
During his service in that body he was on a number of important committees, among which was the Ways and Means, the

Hon. William W. Barr.

(Page 74.)

Judiciary and others. For many years he was a member of the city council. In every office his integrity was unimpeachable. In politics he was a Democrat, and served his party well: as chairman of the county committee, delegate to county and State conventions, as well as a member of the State Central Committee of his party.

He joined the Masons in 1854, and has been one of the most faithful members of the order in that part of the State, filling all of the responsible offices, from a subordinate to Master, and District Grand Master of the counties of Armstrong, Cambria, Clarion, Indiana and Jefferson.

On March 31, 1859, he was married to MARY PRITNER, daughter of Dr. John T. Pritner, a prominent physician of Clarion, by Rev. James Montgomery. Mrs. Barr was born at Curlisville, Pennsylvania, November 22, 1838. Two children were born to them, a son who died in infancy, and a daughter, Lulu Barr, now Mrs. W. A. Hetzel. Mrs Barr makes her home with her daughter.

Hon. W. W. Barr assisted in the formation of the first agricultural society of Clarion County, and was its first secretary. He was a trustee and promoter of the Clarion Normal School. He was a trustee of the Presbyterian Church, and always liberal in his contributions to benevolence.

As though he had not enough of honors, he was appointed by Governor Pattison in July, 1891, as Judge of Clarion County, to fill the vacancy caused by the death of Hon. T. S. Wilson.

He presented the Clarion Bar Association with his fine law library, which was one of the finest in the State, and which will be a monument to his memory in that county forever. He was respected and beloved by every member of the Clarion bar, and acknowledged to be one of the best legal minds in the State. There are some men who make the pathway of their fellow men brighter, and Judge Barr was one of them. He was ever courteous, and a gentleman always. His smiling countenance was a benediction. In him the community has lost a good man and a friend. (Most of the above was gleaned from the *Clarion Republican*, a Clarion paper.)

LULU BARR,[5] daughter of Judge Barr, was married to WILLIAM ALBERT HETZEL September 1, 1885. Mr. Hetzel is engaged in the lumber business, on Wood Street, Pittsburg, Pennsylvania, and their home is at Homewood Avenue and Mead Street, East End Pittsburg, where they have resided for the past seven years. Mrs. Hetzel graduated from Washington Female Seminary, at Washington, Pennsylvania, in 1881. Their children are—

WILLIAM BARR HETZEL,[6] born 1887. He hopes to enter high school next year at the age of fourteen.

CAROLINE HETZEL,[6] born in 1891.

7 ALEXANDER B. BARR.[4]

7 ALEX B. BARR[4] was born in 1828, and died in Punxutawney, Jefferson County, Pennsylvania, November 24, 1893. He was sixty-six years of age. His death was caused by a general breakdown. He was married to Miss KATHERINE LITTLE, a sister of Edward Little, so well known in McAlevy's Fort and in the county, and whose family still resides there. She was born in July, 1841, at McAlevy's Fort.

They had no children of their own, but raised Miss Jennie Barr (now Mrs. Cromer), his brother Thompson's daughter. Mrs. Barr lives at McGees Mills, Pennsylvania, with Mrs. Cromer.

Mr. Barr moved west of the mountains in the spring of 1865. He taught school for a number of years in Stone Valley, Huntingdon County, Pennsylvania. He once wrote the writer, that he did not think there was a youngster in Jackson township of a certain age that had not gone to school to him. After going west of the mountains he engaged in the stone business, in New Bethlehem, Pennsylvania. He continued in that business for several years. The business did not agree with him, and by the advice of his physician he moved up into the pine woods, and lumbered a few years. He was not long in regaining his usual health. His next venture was with his brother Thompson. Together they built a hotel and storeroom in Clarion, Clarion County, Pennsylvania. They did an immense business, and made and lost a great deal of money. They stayed there five or six years, and then he moved to Punxutawney, Pennsylvania. There he bought a large hotel known as the Loomis House. A short time after making the purchase, and paying for it, the town was visited by a disastrous fire, in which his hotel and about fifty other dwellings and buildings went up in smoke in two or three hours' time, with a total loss to him of fifteen thousand dollars. After that time he did not engage in any special business. In 1893 failing health began, and he died of mental and physical prostration in 1894.

When a young man he was much in my father's house. He was a great violinist, and often spent his evenings in that way, much to the delight of the family. He also was one of the finest penmen I have ever seen. He prided himself in it, and was solicited to write sale bills for public auctions. His wife still survives him. She lives at Punxutawney, Pennsylvania.

8 GEORGE BARR.[4]

8 GEORGE BARR[4] was born December 1, 1830, in Center County, Pennsylvania. He married MARY BARR, daughter of Samuel and Jane (McCormick) Barr, of Stone Valley, Huntingdon County, Pennsylvania, April 10, 1856. Her grandfather was David Barr.[2]

Mr. Barr was in the Civil War. He enlisted in Company I, First Missouri M. S. M. Volunteers, in St. Louis, Missouri. He was mustered in in March, 1862, and honorably discharged in April, 1865.

Mrs. Barr was born December 14, 1837. The family moved West in 1859. They live at DeSoto, Missouri. They are both living. He keeps the cemetery at DeSoto.

There were born to them five sons and three daughters.

1 FELICIA JANE BARR[5] married Mr. JAMES WILLEY. They live in DeSoto. Her husband is employed at the machine shops.

2 CLARA F. BARR[5] is at home and is a dressmaker.

3 LAURA HATTIE BARR[5] married Mr. GEORGE D. HOPKINS in 1897. They live in St. Louis, Missouri. He is a cook in a restaurant. They have one son.

GEORGE CLARENCE,[6] born 1899.

4 IRA THOMPSON BARR[5] is a painter by trade. He is single.

5 JOHN ALEXANDER BARR[5] has been in an insane hospital some time, broken down with nervous prostration, which affected his mind, but is improving and will soon be able to return home.

6 HUGH SEMPLE BARR[5] is a brakeman on the Mexican Central Railway, in Mexico. He is single.

7 WILLIAM BARR[5] died January 24, 1884.

8 HUGH M. BARR[5] died November 24, 1872.

The family are all members of the Presbyterian Church, except Mrs. Hopkins, who lifted her letter and united with her husband in the Methodist Episcopal Church.

9 SALLIE BARR.[4]

9 SALLIE BARR[4] was born near Boalsburg, Center County, Pennsylvania, December 21, 1834. She never married, and made her home for some time with her sister, Mrs. Newcomb, and since her sister's death has been keeping house for the boys at their home, 342 Indiana Street, Chicago, Illinois. She taught school for forty-three years, beginning in 1853, and teaching her

Mr. Alex B. Barr.

(Page 76.)

last school in 1896. She taught in Center and Huntingdon Counties. Most of her life was spent in the neighborhood of her home, in that work. She surely is entitled to a life pension for her long and faithful term of service. She always enjoyed her profession, and never had any trouble getting a school, being eminently successful.

She is a splendid scholar, a great reader, a good conversationalist, and a very correct liver. She is a lady of charming manners, and always a welcome visitor among her numerous friends. May her splendid life be as the "path of the just, that shineth more and more unto the perfect day."

10 ASENATH BARR.[4]

10 ASENATH BARR[4] was born February 6, 1837, in Boalsburg, Pennsylvania. She was married to JEFFERSON NEWCOMB, in Mercer County, Pennsylvania, April 10, 1855, at her sister Jane's, where she made her home after her parents' death. While with her sister she attended college at New Wilmington, Pennsylvania. After they were married they removed to Iowa Falls, in 1858. In 1864 they moved to West Union, Iowa, and the same year to Macomb, Illinois. Mr. Newcomb died very suddenly at Keithsburg, Illinois, in 1880. In the same year she moved to Ottumwa, Iowa, where they resided until 1889.

Her son Charles left Ottumwa that year for Chicago, to engage in business, and she went with him and made a home for him. She kept a rooming-house at 342 Indiana Street. She died suddenly with pneumonia June 8, 1900.

We had been in correspondence with her about her family record, but she died before she had sent it. She was much interested in the undertaking.

Mrs. Newcomb caught cold sitting up with a neighbor, and was very bad from the first. She was a healthy woman up to that time. She was one of the kindest mothers and most accommodating neighbors. Her death has been a great loss and shock to her sister Sallie, and to her children. She was a member of the Presbyterian Church for over forty years, a good Christian woman, and beloved by all who knew her. She was buried at Ottumwa on June 11th, from the home of her daughter, Mrs. Lewis.

She left three children, all living.

1 FLORENCE NEWCOMB[6] was born in Boalsburg, Center County, Pennsylvania, April 18, 1856. She taught school for a number of years. She was married to Mr. LEON D. LEWIS, at Ottumwa, Iowa, May 6, 1886. He was born in Ottumwa and raised there. His occupation is a traveling auditor for the Western Railway Association. To them were born three children.

Twins were born July 12, 1887, and died July 13, 1887.

MABLE NEWCOMB LEWIS[6] was born February 8, 1889.

2 WILLIAM BARR NEWCOMB[6] was born January 15, 1858, at Iowa Falls, Iowa. He married Miss MAY RASMUSSEN, of Racine, Wisconsin, in 1892. He is occupied in the commission business, Chicago, Illinois. They have two children, both boys.

HAROLD NEWCOMB,[6] born in October, 1894.

ORVILLE NEWCOMB,[6] born in 1896.

3 CHARLES CARMAN NEWCOMB[6] was born June 21, 1868, at Macomb, Illinois. He is single, and is employed as cashier in a wholesale grocery house in the city of Chicago. The writer is very much indebted to him not only for such a good history of the family, but for some valuable facts concerning our early ancestors, which he took the pains to look up for this history.

This concludes the family of WILLIAM BARR,[3] third son of DAVID BARR,[2] and shows them to have been a most interesting, intellectual, and highly respectable and cultured family; and will be a chapter that will be read with much satisfaction by the friends. They have all made their mark in the world.

IV SAMUEL BARR.[3]

4 SAMUEL BARR,[3] son of DAVID and SARAH THOMPSON BARR, was born in Center County, Pennsylvania, and died quite young.

V JOHN BARR.[3]

5 JOHN BARR[3] was also born in Center County, Pennsylvania. He married Miss NANCY BRISBIN, a sister of his brother Robert's wife, but died soon after in a mysterious way. None of his friends ever knew how he died.

VI POLLY BARR.[3]

6 POLLY BARR[3] was born in Center County, Pennsylvania. She married Mr. GEORGE McCORMICK. They had one son and two daughters. The names of the daughters were Jane and Margaret.

> JANE McCORMICK[4] married SAMUEL BARR of Stone Valley, Huntingdon County, Pennsylvania, son of SAMUEL and LYDIA BARR. She died in Stone Valley. (See SAMUEL BARR's record for further notice.)

> MARGARET BARR McCORMICK[4] married Mr. MILLER and lived in Ohio. Nothing more is known of her.

VII JENNIE BARR.[3]

7 JENNIE BARR[3] married DAVID WHITEHILL. They had no family. They both died many years ago.

VIII MARGARET BARR.[3]

8 MARGARET BARR[3] married ADAM MILLER and lived in Center County, Pennsylvania. They had four sons and four daughters.

MARY MILLER,[4] the eldest daughter, married Mr. HARTS-
WICK, of Boalsburg, Pennsylvania.

HARRY MILLER,[4] one of the sons, is the only one of the
family living, and he is eighty-seven years of age and
lives at Boalsburg, Pennsylvania.

IX MARY BARR.[3]

9 MARY BARR[3] is the last of DAVID BARR's[2] family.   Of
her we could learn nothing.

We are sorry the records of this family are fragmentary and
incomplete, but the records of some of the families being lost
or burned, and the older people of the connection having about
all died, it was impossible to get a satisfactory account of them.
If anything should come in later, you will find it in the Supplement, at the back of the book.

Mrs. Asenath Barr.

(Page 79.)

FAMILY III.

WILLIAM BARR.[2]

WILLIAM BARR,[2] the third son of Great-grandfather ROBERT BARR,[1] married Miss ANNA TODD in Ireland, and had some family before coming to this country with his father and rest of the family in 1790. His eldest son's name was Robert, as mentioned in the will, but further than this we have been unable to get any trace of the family. If any one into whose hands this history may fall, knows anything of them or any of their descendants, we will be glad if they will notify us to that effect. They may have gone back to Ireland.

FAMILY IV.

SAMUEL BARR.[2]

Our Grandfather Samuel Barr[2] was born in Donegal County, Ireland, in 1757. He died October 12, 1848, at the ripe old age of ninety-one. None of his children or brothers ever attained to his years, so far as we know.

He kept a diary of each day, which he began in 1789, the year before they left Ireland, and from which we have gleaned much valuable information about the family. This diary is bound in ledger form, is well written, and shows him to have been a very fair scholar, and a man of more than average intelligence. The memoirs are in possession of Aunt Elizabeth Anderson's heirs, of Indiana, Pennsylvania. It is highly prized by the family, and will be more so by coming generations. It is indeed a pity that he destroyed a large part of it, using the paper (which was scarce in those days) for shoe patterns, as he made the shoes for the family; and what a task he must have had of it. He destroyed parts of it that would have been a most valuable aid to us in getting up this history.

He married Lydia Black, of Jackson township, Huntingdon County, Pennsylvania. She was born in 1777, and was therefore twenty years younger than he. They were married Tuesday, May 20, 1800, by Rev. Mather Stephens. He was therefore forty-three years of age when he married. Although there was a difference of twenty years in their ages, she died first, on September 24, 1843, at the age of sixty-six. She was quite an invalid, suffering much from rheumatism, and confined to her chair for several years, but remarkably cheerful through it all.

We can trace her people back for two generations. Her grandmother's name was Lydia Hunter; her mother's name was

The House and Landscape.

(Page 85.)

Lydia Black. They lived in Ireland, not far from the Barr settlement, and when they came to this country they resided in Stone Valley, neighbors to grandfather. Grandmother had two brothers, Daniel and James Black. As game abounded in those days, the story is told that Daniel Black killed seven wild turkeys at one shot. He loaded with shot, and when he heard them coming, he hid behind a log; and when they came near and discovered him they ran together to fly, and he shot among them, killing so many he could not carry them home.

Grandfather Barr owned and cultivated two hundred acres of land one-half mile north-east of McAlevy's Fort, on the public road leading to the upper end of the valley. Most of the land was somewhat hilly, but excellent producing land. There was a fine spring of limestone water near the house and also a well of the same kind of water in the spring-house at the door. The house, which was built by Great-grandfather Barr soon after he came to the valley, is still standing. It has housed five generations of Barr's. The house was built in 1796, and so is one hundred and four years old. It was a substantial two-story log house, well built, large and commodious. There was a porch along the whole length of the house, but it was taken away when the house was repaired. The house has been weather-boarded and looks quite modern. Samuel Barr after he was married went to housekeeping in this house and lived here fifty years of his married life and one year as a widower. It is still occupied by the widow of Grandfather Barr's youngest son (Daniel), Mrs. Martha Barr, and her son Joseph, who farms the old homestead. Mrs. Barr has lived in the house fifty-three years, or ever since her marriage. We are glad it is still in the Barr connection. The barn is a large frame barn, well built, and can be seen to the left of the picture. The picture was taken from the east and across Stone Creek, which runs in front of the house. This is the principal stream of the valley.

The barn was the first frame barn in the township, and was used for church services before there were any churches in the community. It was erected by grandfather in 1831. The most of the roof and the weather-boarding are the first that were put on.

Here they lived and died, as did their father and mother, and were buried in the graveyard on the farm, as previously noted. It is a beautiful location and a historic spot, and very dear to some of us as containing the dust of our dear and worthy ancestors.

They were members of the Associate Church (now the United Presbyterian), and brought up their family very strictly in that faith. The Rev. Samuel Easton was their pastor at their death, remaining there as such for nineteen years. He was followed by Rev. John M. Adair, who was pastor for thirty years. Great-grandfather was one of the founders of that church, which is one hundred years old.

Grandfather Barr belonged to the old Whig party, was a strong anti-slavery man, and had the courage of his convictions.

Their lives were lives of great toil and sacrifice. They began life in a new country, where the inhabitants were few and far between; amid great forests of pine, hemlock and oak. They had to cut and clear their own land and put up their own buildings. It was a task to clear these great forests and build the fences, and hence furnished abundant exercise for his large family of boys and girls (for the girls worked much beside their brothers in the field). They made their own clothes, mostly linen and woolen. They raised the flax, bleached, broke, scrutched, carded, and spun it, requiring a vast amount of labor. The girls had a very prominent part in this work, and it did not seem to hurt them, for they all lived to a good old age. The youngest, Aunt Elizabeth Anderson, is still living, but over eighty years of age. The wheat was sown among the stumps, and

Rev. James Thomas Wilson.

(Page 92.)

reaped with hand-sickles (a short steal hook with teeth). The boys and girls side by side cut their swath of grain. It must have been an interesting sight. Some of those hooks are still in our possession, interesting relics of a past age. Those were strange days, to us as we look back from our times. They had about twenty miles to drive to market with their grain and produce. They drove heavy wagons with blue, English beds, and six fine horses; started with eighty bushels of grain, and took two days to make the trip to Lewiston across Stone Mountain, or to Huntingdon, the former being the better grain market. This was before railroads were even thought of, and only canals were used. So that with our machinery and improved modes of travel, we accomplish more in less time and live much faster than they, but do we live better?

The boys now crowd into the cities and enter a profession or an office. The girls teach school, play the piano, work at fancy work, or do office work. Perhaps the change is better, perhaps not. But better to be out of the world than not to keep up with the procession. We must adapt ourselves to the times in which we live, or be laughed at and die unnoticed and uncared for. But the men and women of those days, inured to hardship and toughened by toil, laid the foundation of a strong physical manhood and womanhood, and stalwart character, which fitted them for becoming the parents of strong, noble sons and daughters. Are we as well fitted as they, by our changed conditions, to transmit to our posterity health of body, mind and soul? Are we the worthy sons and daughters of these strong and worthy ancestors? Our own hearts must answer, and each heart for itself. The test of the judgment bar will tell.

To this worthy couple, strong of will and strong of faith, were born six sons and five daughters, all living to manhood and womanhood, all marrying, and all heads of respectable families, several of whom occupy influential places in the church and the world. They are as follows:

  I MARY BARR.[3]
  II LYDIA BARR.[3]
  III ROBERT BARR.[3]
  IV JANE BARR.[3]
  V SAMUEL BARR.[3]
  VI JAMES BARR.[3]
  VII GABRIEL BARR.[3]
  VIII MARGARET BARR.[3]
  IX DAVID BARR.[3]
  X ELIZABETH BARR.[3]
  XI DANIEL BARR.[3]

I MARY BARR.[3]

1 MARY BARR[3] was born March 22, 1801. She was married to JOHN OSBORN in 1825. She died in June, 1835. He died in 1854. They lived near McAlevy's Fort, Huntingdon County, Pennsylvania, on a farm. They were blessed with five children.

  1 LYDIA JANE OSBORN.[4]
  2 JOHN T. OSBORN.[4]
  3 SAMUEL B. OSBORN.[4]
  4 NANCY E. OSBORN.[4]
  5 MARY C. OSBORN.[4]

1 LYDIA JANE OSBORN.[4]

1 LYDIA JANE OSBORN[4] was born November 27, 1825. She was married to Mr. JAMES PLATT in December, 1855, in Mifflin County, by Rev. John S. Easton. Mr. Pratt was born April 29, 1830, in Mifflin County, Pennsylvania.

Mr. Platt enlisted in a company called the Jackson Artillery in 1859, of which Mr. Grossman was captain. On September 19th, he came over to Lewiston to attend an encampment, and

Mrs. Jennie Wilson.

(Page 92.)

with a Mr. McStewart he went to town to buy some oysters. As he returned, Edward Mills, who was standing guard, shot him. He had his gun loaded with a tenpenny cut nail, and he claimed that he stumbled into a hole and the gun went off. The nail went through Mr. Platt, and killed him. He died September 22, 1859, three days after he was shot. The company buried him in Mifflin County, and bore all the expenses.

Mrs. Platt and her two children were living at McAlevy's Fort at the time. The third child was born three months after Mr. Platt's death.

1 MARY ELIZABETH PLATT[5] was born in Mifflin County, May 18, 1856, and died January 10, 1860, and was buried near McAlevy's Fort, Pennsylvania.

2 THOMAS MARION PLATT[5] was born May 25, 1857. He was married in Illinois, May 3, 1892, to Miss ANNIE BROOKS, but only lived a year or so with her. They had no children. He lives near Macomb, Illinois. He went West in 1883.

3 SARAH MARGARET PLATT[5] was born December 20, 1859. She married SAMUEL STEWART, of Logan, Mifflin County, Pennsylvania, November 12, 1875. They have separated. She lives in Pittsburg, and keeps boarders for a living. She has one son.

SAMUEL CORNELIUS STEWART[6] was born October 21, 1876. He went blind last March, and has been in the Pennsylvania Hospital in Philadelphia. After an operation he could see but little. So her only support is a care to her. Surely some people have their own troubles.

Mrs. Platt moved to Mifflin County, and married AARON RIDEN in 1867. They lived for several years on a farm on the Reedsville pike. They moved west on March 14, 1877. She had no family by her second husband.   Her children Sarah and Thomas did not go west with her.   Sarah moved to Pittsburg November 8, 1887.   Her address is 710 Watson Street.

Mr. Riden died soon after going west to Illinois.   Mrs. Riden died August 9, 1900, of a rupture.   She suffered intensely for weeks.   She had an operation performed, and died in the operation; but she could not have lived anyway.   She was buried at Galesburg, Illinois.

2 JOHN T. OSBORN.[4]

2 JOHN T. OSBORN,[4] second child of MARY (BARR) OSBORN,[3] was born December 11, 1827, near McAlevy's Fort, Pennsylvania.   He married H. M. AILKINS, January 3, 1856, and lived near Siglerville, Mifflin County, Pennsylvania, on a farm.   There all his family were born.

He moved west some years ago to the neighborhood where his sister, Mrs. Rider, lived.   His wife died and left three sons. Mr. Osborn has had three strokes of paralysis and cannot speak, but can write a little.   He lives at Macomb, Illinois.   The sons are as follows.

> JAMES M. OSBORN,[5] born August 6, 1858, is married, and lives in Galesburg, Illinois.   He has one son.   He is a machinist.

> WILLIAM T. OSBORN,[5] born September 15, 1860, is married, and lives in Kansas City, Missouri.   They have no children.   He is an electrician.

> ELMER R. OSBORN,[5] born July 25, 1866, is at home at present attending his father, but lives in Kansas City. He is single.   He is a machinist, and works with his brother.   The boys all have good positions.

3 SAMUEL B. OSBORN.[4]

3 SAMUEL B. OSBORN[4] was born July 4, 1830.   He married MARTHA TREASTER.   They have no children.   They live in

Prof. J. Given Thompson.

(Page 94.)

Doddsville, Illinois. They run a grocery store. Mrs. Osborn is getting feeble.

4 NANCY E. OSBORN.[4]

4 NANCY E. OSBORN[4] was born in 1832.

5 MARY C. OSBORN.[4]

5 MARY C. OSBORN[4] was born in 1835.

Mr. Osborn[3] after aunt's death married for his second wife Miss RANEY, of Center County. They had one son.

> CHARLEY H. OSBORN. He has six children: Laura, Elliott, William, Roy, James and Marjery. They live near Belleville, Center County, Pennsylvania.

II LYDIA BARR.[3]

2 LYDIA BARR[3] was born October 5, 1802, on the homestead, near McAlevy's Fort, Huntingdon County, Pennsylvania. She was married to SAMUEL REED December 1, 1825. Mr. Reed was born January 12, 1793, south of Huntingdon County, Pennsylvania, and brought up his family there. He was an energetic and successful farmer, and took a leading part in the affairs of the neighborhood where he lived. He was a faithful member and an efficient elder of the Associate Church of Huntingdon. He died October, 1860, on the farm where he lived. His wife died September, 1878, aged seventy-six years.

After Mr. Reed's death, Mrs. Reed for thirteen years before her death made her home with her daughter, Mrs Harris, at Lacona, Iowa, where Rev. Harris was settled at the time. She died in peace, with a confident trust in her Saviour. They were a most pious and godly couple, and raised a large and most excellent family.

Their children are as follows:

1 JENNIE REED.[4]
2 JOHN M. REED.[4]
3 LYDIA REED.[4]
4 REV. SAMUEL B. REED, D. D.[4]
5 ROBERT H. REED, M. D.[4]
6 MARY A. REED.[4]
7 JAMES REED.[4]
8 DAVID REED.[4]
9 MARTHA REED.[4]
10 DANIEL REED.[4]
11 WILLIAM E. REED, M. D.[4]

1 JENNIE REED.[4]

1 JENNIE REED[4] was born September 27, 1826. She was educated at Washington Seminary and taught school a while. She was married to Rev. J. T. WILSON September 22, 1853, by Rev. Thos. Hanna, D. D. They spent many happy years together. They had no children.

Cousin Jennie died July 27, 1879, in New York city, where her husband was settled at the time. She was a most faithful and efficient helper to her husband in his domestic and pastoral life, until she heard the call of the Master to come up higher. Her husband writing of her says: "Her's was a beautiful life of conscientious devotion in the discharge of all relative and religious duties." A worthy tribute of regard from one who knew her best.

Cousin Wilson was born November 14, 1830. He was educated in Washington College, and studied theology at Allegheny Seminary. He was licensed August 23, 1859, by Allegheny Presbytery, and ordained January 2, 1861, by Conemaugh Presbytery. He was pastor of Taylorsville and connections from January, 1861, to December, 1861; of First Church, Brooklyn, New York, July 17, 1862, to March 11, 1867; of Parker

Rev. J. W. Harris.
(Page 96.)

Samuel B. Harris, M. D.

City, Armstrong County, Pennsylvania, September 23, 1874, to March 31, 1878; of East 116th Street, New York City, June 6, 1879, to August 17, 1881. After this he was stated supply for two years in Topeka, Kansas. He was pastor at Sidney, Ohio, April 11, 1882 to December 5, 1882; stated supply at Greenwich, New York, 1886. Brother Wilson is a good preacher and a genial man. He married for his second wife, Miss MARY ISOPHINE MOORE, daughter of Dr. D. D. Moore, of Xenia, Ohio, March 1, 1881. Dr. Moore was an elder in the First United Presbyterian Church for many years before his death. He led the choir when the writer was a member of the choir in 1875, while attending the Theological Seminary in that place; also during the pasorate of the writer. They own and are running Wilson Hall in connection with Cooper Memorial College, Sterling, Kansas.

2 JOHN M. REED.[4]

2 JOHN M. REED[4] was born March 29, 1828. He worked on the farm until he became of age. He then went into the mercantile business for a while, but feeling that he ought to have more education, gave that up and entered Westminster College, and remained there for a time. He then married MAGGIE E. MOOR, of Granville, Illinois, in 1858, and tried farming, but still felt impressed with the thought that he ought to study for the ministry. So he moved to Monmouth, and entered the college there. But the second year after he entered his health failed and he went down with consumption. He died July 4, 1864. He departed rejoicing in the Saviour, and although not permitted to carry out his purpose, was willing and ready to depart. He left a wife and one daughter, Lydia M. (now Mrs. J. Given Thompson), to mourn his death. His wife married again, but has since followed him to that better country.

LYDIA M. REED.[5]

LYDIA M. REED[5] was born February 8, 1860, at Monmouth, Illinois. She married Prof. J. GIVEN THOMPSON—son of Rev. S. F. Thompson, who lives at Oxford, Ohio—June 1, 1887.

Prof. Thompson comes of a preacher family. His mother was Ellen Given, sister of Rev. James Given, of Brookville, Pennsylvania. He is a brother of Rev. Pressly Thompson, of Colorado Springs, Prof. E. P. Thompson of Miami University, and Rev. Joseph A. Thompson, D. D., President of Tarkio College. Prof. Thompson is Professor of Mathematics in Cooper Memorial College, Sterling, Kansas. He took a post-graduate course in Ann Arbor, Michigan, and the University of Columbia, with the degree of A. M. He graduated at Monmouth in 1885. He is considered a good professor and a handsome man. They have a pleasant home, and are a very happy family.

Mrs. Thompson is the sixth Lydia in succession in the connection, and like all her Aunt Reeds, married a man her junior, which we have heard is a sign of wealth. We hope it will be true in their case; if not in gold and silver, at least in the riches of heaven, "which neither moth nor rust doth corrupt, nor thieves break through and steal." Their children consist of—

PAUL DEAN THOMPSON,[6] born April 26, 1888.

SAMUEL BARR REED THOMPSON,[6] born December 11, 1889.

PHILIP EDWARD THOMPSON,[6] born June 11, 1890.

ALLEN KERR THOMPSON,[6] born March 9, 1895.

These are four bright, interesting lads. The first two are great readers.

3 LYDIA REED.[4]

3 LYDIA REED[4] was born July 3, 1829. She was educated at Washington Seminary, and taught school for several terms. The writer's first days at public school were under her direction. I do not know that she was particularly proud of her pupil.

Rev. Daniel Harris.

(Page 95.)

Mrs. Lydia Reed Harris.

(Page 94.)

She went to Monmouth the next year after Uncle Reed's death, in 1861. The family moved there in 1862. She got the first letter the writer ever wrote, and we can remember her saying, "You are the youngest correspondent I have ever had." She was a good teacher, but Rev. DANIEL HARRIS made her acquaintance, and at his invitation she decided to make a change of occupation and become the mistress of his home, and the partner of his joys and sorrows. So on May 3, 1864, at Monmouth, Illinois, they were united in marriage.

Rev. Harris was born June 14, 1835, in Clinton County, Indiana. He graduated from Monmouth College in 1862, and studied Theology at Monmouth; was licensed April 2, 1863, by Monmouth Presbytery, and ordained and installed as pastor of the United Presbyterian congregation at Fountain Green, Illinois, by the same Presbytery, August 2, 1864. He remained there until December 28, 1869. He became pastor at Lacona, Warren County, Iowa, November 7, 1870, and remained there until November 15, 1877. He was principal at the Lacona Academy of that place. He became pastor of Ryegate, Vermont, February 9, 1886; was pastor at Mundale, New York, for several years, demitting his charge in January, 1900.

To them were born three children, two sons and one daughter.

1 JENNIE E. HARRIS.[5]
2 REV. J. W. HARRIS.[5]
3 SAMUEL BARR HARRIS.[5]

1 JENNIE E. HARRIS.[5]

1 JENNIE E. HARRIS[5] was born January 14, 1866. She was unusually bright, and in early childhood seemed to be a subject of grace, and united with the church in her ninth year. She was aiming to prepare herself for a missionary, and was developing a lovely Christian character, but God was preparing her for

the home above, and took her to himself in her sixteenth year, July 9, 1881.

2 REV. J. W. HARRIS.[5]

2 Rev. J. W. Harris[5] was born October 7, 1867. He graduated from Monmouth College in the class of 1890; attended Allegheny Seminary, and graduated with honors in 1894. He settled as pastor of Greensboro (Vermont) congregation, Vermont Presbytery, the same year, where he labored for over six years. But the climate proved too severe for him and he was obliged to try a change. Consequently he took a trip with his wife to Cuba in January, 1900, where he spent part of the winter and was much improved in health, and returned to New York in March. He has a fine lecture on Cuba, with stereopticon views of the people and the scenery. Cousin J. W. Harris was married to MARY A. YOUNG, March 3, 1896. They have no children.

3 SAMUEL BARR HARRIS.[5]

3 Samuel Barr Harris[5] was born May 26, 1873, at Lacona, Iowa. He attended St. Johnsberry Academy and Monmouth College; worked at the electric business for a while; then feeling that God was calling him to the work of a medical missionary, he went to Philadelphia, and entered the Medico-Surgical College, and graduated May 26, 1899. He went as a medical missionary to Columbia, South America, with Rev. Norwood, a Bible agent who had been there for twenty years. They sailed August 19, 1899, arriving September 11, 1899. A terrible war broke out there in October, the next month after they arrived, and there were many battles. He has had his hands full and has had a wonderful experience in surgical work. He is doing much missionary work there in connection with his medical practice, and is doing much good by scattering tracts and giving out Bibles to any who will receive them, and talking

Rev. Samuel B. Reed, D. D.

(Page 97.)

with the people about the Saviour.   He is reported as doing a
wonderful work among the soldiers, and has the reputation of
being the best surgeon in Columbia.   Many are anxious to
learn about his religion.

4 REV. SAMUEL BARR REED, D. D.[4]

4 REV. SAMUEL B. REED[4] was born near Huntingdon,
Pennsylvania, June 6, 1831.   He early expressed a desire for
the ministry, and was accordingly educated with that object in
view.   He graduated from Franklin College in 1853, and
studied theology at Canonsburg, Pennsylvania, and Xenia,
Ohio.   He was licensed to preach May 16, 1856, by Philadelphia Presbytery, and ordained by Allegheny Presbytery April 29,
1857.   He was pastor of the First United Presbyterian Church,
Pittsburg, Pennsylvania, from April, 1857, to July 11, 1859.
The First Church divided and organized the Fifth Church, and
he accepted their call and was pastor from February 28, 1860,
to March 31, 1874.   He was stated supply at Evans, Colorado,
from 1874 to 1876.   After regaining his health there, he was
elected president of Knoxville College, Knoxville, Tennessee.
He remained there from 1877 to 1881.   He was also Professor
of Theology in Knoxville College during his presidency.
Again he went to Evans, Colorado, where he was pastor from
April 7, 1882, to April 6, 1883.   He supplied at Davenport,
Iowa, until his death, April 10, 1884.   He was fifty-three years
of age at the time of his death.   He died in full assurance
of faith.

He was married to MARY J. LACKEY February 12, 1857,
at her home in Freeport, Illinois.   They had no children.
Mrs. Reed is still living in Chicago, Illinois.   She has been
matron of a children's home in Chicago for sixteen years.

Dr. Reed's publications are a tract, "A Sinner Saved;" an
address, "The Polished Jewel;" a lecture on "Pastoral Visita-

tion;" a "Thanksgiving Sermon," and numerous articles in the religious papers.

Dr. Reed was a very pious man, a faithful student, and a most instructive and interesting preacher. He had a style of address peculiarly his own, which held the attention of his hearers to the last word. He was a very kind-hearted man, and much beloved. His was a very busy life, and overwork hastened his end.

5 ROBERT H. REED, M. D.[4]

5 ROBERT H. REED[4] was born September 26, 1832, near Huntingdon, Pennsylvania.

He was a humble, good man, very much respected and beloved by all who knew him. He studied medicine in Keo_ kuk, Iowa. He first practiced in Illinois, then removed to Arkansas City, Kansas, where they resided for many years. He died April 20, 1899, at Sharon, Harper County, Kansas, where he was living at that time. He was regarded as a skilful physician.

He was married to M. J. WATT January 19, 1858. Dr. Reed was an elder in the United Presbyterian Church and a faithful worker. His death was very sudden and unexpected. He awoke in the night with heart trouble, and was gone in a few minutes. He had but one son, Samuel Barr Reed.[5]

SAMUEL BARR REED.[5]

SAMUEL BARR REED[5] was born in 1862. He married Miss ANNA HUTCHISON, daughter of Mr. and Mrs. J. W. Hutchison, of Arkansas City, Kansas, August 10, 1882. Mrs. Reed was born in 1863. They live near Attica, Kansas, on a fine farm. His mother makes her home with him. They have five promising sons.

Robert H. Reed, M. D.

(Page 98.)

ILA REED.[6]

STACY B. REED.[6]

VERNE REED.[6]

EULA REED.[6]

ROBERT H. REED.[6]

6 MARY A. REED.[4]

6 MARY A. REED[4] was born August 31, 1834. She attended Washington Seminary, and was married to D. D. PARRY, of Xenia, Ohio, at Monmouth Illinois, March 24, 1864. They resided at Monmouth until 1888, when they moved to Arkansas City, Kansas, where Judge Parry died January 4, 1895, of apoplexy.

Daniel Dean Parry was a good business man, and much esteemed by all who knew him. He enlisted as a private soldier during the Civil War, on April 19, 1861. He enlisted in Company F, Third Ohio Volunteer Infantry (three-months men), and on June following was mustered into the three-year service in the same company and regiment. His final discharge was dated at Camp Dennison, March 1, 1863. While in the service he spent his first six months in West Virginia, went south with the Army of the Ohio, and returned with Buell. At Perryville, Kentucky, October 8, 1862, a ball penetrated his left knee, which led to the amputation of the limb twenty-five hours later.

He arrived at Monmouth, Illinois, March 23, 1863, and the next day was given a position as deputy county clerk. He held this place about three years, and in November, 1867, was elected county treasurer, an office which he held for four terms in succession. In 1870 he was elected as a member of the State Board of Equalization, and for four years discharged the duties of the two offices. In 1880 he represented Warren County in the Illinois legislature for two terms. He was in the real estate and insurance business in Monmouth until 1888, when he with his family removed to Arkansas City, Kansas. In 1891 he was elected justice of the peace of Arkansas City, and in 1894 he was elected Probate Judge of Cowly County, which office he was just about to enter when called away suddenly by death, January 5, 1895. His life was an active public life. He was a man of unswerving integrity; pure in his private life, and unblemished in his public career. He was a Republican in politics.

Judge Parry and his wife were both members of the United Presbyterian Church at Monmouth, Illinois, and Arkansas City, Kansas.

Mrs. Parry is now residing at Long Beach, California. She has three children.

    1 NETTIE ADALINE PARRY.[5]
    2 WALTER DEAN PARRY.[5]
    3 JESSIE MAY PARRY.[5]

1 NETTIE ADALINE PARRY.[5]

1 NETTIE ADALINE PARRY[6] was born at Monmouth, Illinois, February 19, 1865. She was married in Arkansas City, Kansas, October 13, 1891, to EMMETT P. REYNOLDS. They have two children, both girls.

    HELEN MAE REYNOLDS,[6] born at Arkansas City, Kansas, October 16, 1892.

    MARY PARRY REYNOLDS,[6] born at Arkansas City, Kansas, August 1, 1897.

2 WALTER DEAN PARRY.[5]

2 WALTER DEAN PARRY,[5] born at Monmouth, Illinois, May 5, 1867. He was married to ANNA PATTON at Arkansas City, October 9, 1890. They have had four children.

    HAROLD DEAN PARRY,[6] born at South Haven, Kansas, January 16, 1893, died at Arkansas City, July 12, 1894.

Hon. Daniel Dean Parry.

(Page 99.)

RAYMOND PATTON PARRY,[6] born at Arkansas City, July 7, 1895.

MILDRED LAURETTA PARRY,[6] born at Arkansas City, September 28, 1897, died at Arkansas City, August 15, 1899.

DONALD DEAN PARRY,[6] born at Arkansas City, October 5, 1899.

3 JESSIE MAY PARRY.[5]

3 JESSIE MAY PARRY[5] was born at Monmouth, Illinois, April 8, 1869. She is living at present with her mother, Mrs. Mary Parry, at Long Beach, California.

Walter D. Parry[5] and his brother-in-law, Emmett P. Reynolds, are in business together at Blackwell, Oklahoma, Territory. They keep a shoe and men's furnishing store.

The Parry family are all quite musical. Judge Parry played the violin, and Mrs. Parry, his wife, is a good singer. Mrs. Nettie Reynolds plays the piano, violin, and mandolin. Walter plays the cornet and guitar, and also teaches music. Emmett Reynolds plays the guitar.

All the children, son-in-law and daughter-in-law, are members of the United Presbyterian Church. This is certainly a fine family record. If all the families of the world were like this one, what a paradise this world would be. Nothing but the grace and righteousness of Christ can make it so.

7 JAMES REED.[4]

7 JAMES REED[4] was born February 26, 1837. He was a good, steady boy and very promising, but was called home when about fifteen years of age, February 20, 1853.

8 DAVID REED.[4]

8 DAVID REED[4] was born March 8, 1839. He was a bright child, but died of scarlet fever when about five years of age.

9 MARTHA REED.[4]

9 MARTHA REED[4] was born April 28, 1841. She was quiet and retiring in her disposition. She loved to read, but cared little for company. She died in Monmouth, December 9, 1893.

10 DANIEL REED.[4]

10 DANIEL REED[4] was born October 29, 1843. He enlisted in a company of soldiers composed mostly of students, who went from Monmouth for one hundred days' service in the Civil War, in June, 1864. He died of camp fever at Fort Leavenworth, Kansas, August 9, 1864. His remains were taken to Granville, Illinois, where his mother and brother Robert were at that time, and interred in the Granville cemetery.

Before starting he realized the possibility of never returning, and remarked that if he was to die in the army, it would be as well there as anywhere. The Sacrament of the Lord's Supper was celebrated in First Church, Monmouth, on the Sabbath before the company started. Dr. D. A. Wallace, the president of the college, gave the soldiers an earnest address in the afternoon. Cousin Daniel remarked that he was glad they had the Communion before starting out.

After he got sick and was taken to the hospital, a kind lady asked him if he had any message to send home to his mother. He replied, "Not much; my mother knows I trust in Jesus." He was not only a Union soldier, but a soldier of Christ.

11 WILLIAM E. REED.[4]

11 WILLIAM E. REED, M. D.,[4] was born July 20, 1846. He went to the army in a company from Huntingdon, Pennsylvania, in 1862, and served in the Civil War with Company F, 125th Regiment Pennsylvania Volunteer Infantry. He served

William E. Reed, M. D.

(Page 102.)

most of the time in 1862-63 in the Army of the Potomac, engaging in the battles of South Mountain, Antietam, Fredericksburg, and Chancellorsville or the Wilderness. He enlisted for nine months, but served overtime. He never received a scratch during that time. His health being very much impaired by exposure, he came home when discharged, to his mother, who had removed in the meantime to Monmouth, Illinois. But he soon become restless, and reenlisted as one of the veteran con_ tingent, to fill up the then much depleted Eleventh Illinois Infantry Regiment, Company E, in the winter of 1863–64, and served to the close of the war.

After he returned to Monmouth he attended college a while, and then went to the Soldiers' College, at Fulton, Illinois. He graduated in medicine and surgery at the Missouri College of Physicians and Surgeons, at St. Joseph. He began the practice of medicine at Winterset, Iowa. He was frozen out there the first winter, and drifted south to Kansas City, Missouri; but was driven out of there by malaria, and from thence he removed to Los Angeles, California, where he has practiced for about nineteen years, and still makes his home there. At this writing he is traveling for his health, and is at Cape Nome, Alaska.

While practicing medicine in Missouri, he married Miss ADELIA M. PELTIET, on November 12, 1874. She was born in Champlain, Clinton County, New York, October 19, 1851, and is a Daughter of the American Revolution, being a descendant of Captain Antoine Pauliut, who served throughout the American Revolution.

They have two children, both bright and promising.

LENA REED.[5]

WILLIAM REED.[5]

This closes the record of the Reed family: and while it is lengthy, it is very interesting, because it was a remarkable family; remarkable for its piety, and its prominence in public, civil, and religious works.

III ROBERT BARR.[2]

3 ROBERT BARR,[2] the eldest son of Grandfather SAMUEL BARR,[2] was born May 29, 1804, in Barre Township, Huntingdon County, Pennsylvania. He was married three times. He married JANE McMINN April 12, 1838. She was born April 7, 1816, in Potter township, Center County, Pennsylvania. They were hard-working, industrious people. Few men have stood as much hard work as Uncle Robert. He worked with his father until he was thirty-four years of age; then married, and bought the farm just outside of McAlevy's Fort, adjoining the old homestead. He owned an excellent farm.

He erected a grist-mill at the fort, put up a high dam, and put an over-shot wheel in his mill, which backed the water so it interfered with his brother Gabriel, who had a saw-mill and tannery just above. This made some trouble. Uncle Gabriel sold out and left for the West, and the saw-mill and tannery were permitted to go down. The mill built by Uncle Robert is still standing and in use. It has been of great service to the community. He sold the farm and mill and moved to the back part of the valley, two and a half miles west. But this was a bad move. He bought two farms and had more land, but much poorer land. He also bought a grist-mill and saw-mill with the farms. He built a fine barn on each farm, and made many other improvements. He then sold one of these farms, and lived on the other for a while, and then sold it and bought a home and built another grist-mill almost in sight of the old homestead where he was born. He died there February 14, 1880, in his seventy-sixth year. His wife died suddenly, November 18, 1860, in her forty-fifth year. To this union were born six children.

1 ANNA BARR.[4]

2 SAMUEL BARR,[4] born July 2, 1841, died August 7, 1851.

3 Infant, died February 10, 1844, aged eleven days.

4 Infant, died March 20, 1845, aged eleven days.

5 WILLIAM BARR,[4] born April 3, 1846, died March 27, 1851.

6 THOMAS BARR.[4]

1 ANNA BARR.[4]

1 ANNA BARR[4] was born February 1, 1839. She attended Westminster College, and while there met M. S. TELFORD, to whom she was married July 8, 1863, by Rev. J. M. Adair, at her home.

She was a prudent woman of excellent judgment, and made one of the kindest of mothers and a good minister's wife. She died July 29, 1896, at Homer City, Pennsylvania, of paralysis, after two weeks' illness. She raised a model family and lived to see them occupying honorable places in the church.

Rev. M. S. Telford, her husband, was born July 3, 1834, in Hebron, Washington County, New York. He is a brother of the late Rev. John C. Telford, D. D. He graduated at Westminster College in 1861, and studied theology at Xenia, Ohio, and Allegheny, Pennsylvania. He was licensed April, 1863, by Conemaugh Presbytery, and ordained June 16, 1864, by the same. He was pastor of Jacksonville and Crete, Indiana County, Pennsylvania, 1864 to 1872; Beaver Run and Cherry Run, Jefferson County, Pennsylvania, February, 1873, to April 12, 1882; Hanover, Beaver County, Pennsylvania, 1882 to 1888; Wurtemburg and Camp Run, 1888 to 1896; Homer City and Crete (where he started first), 1896 to the present time. He is a fine preacher and a soul-winner, and has been very successful. He is a man of good evangelistic spirit and methods, and keeps up to the times. He has just completed a new church in the Crete branch of his charge.

He was associated with the writer in starting the Ellwood City (Pennsylvania) congregation and building the present church. It was built in a new field and a new city, before there was any congregation, and was paid for when dedicated, September, 1891. There is now a self-supporting church there, with Rev. D. M. Cleland as pastor.

The writer's mother once said when he was preparing for the ministry, "If you could preach as well as Mr. Telford, I would be glad to see you in the ministry." We may say we have held many very precious seasons together in social fellowship, and in evangelistic meetings, with this preacher cousin. Some of the most wonderful manifestations of Holy Ghost power we have ever witnessed, was when associated with him in a series of meetings. We owe much to him, and are thankful that he married into the family.

Few men have more to be thankful for, in his good wife, in his family, and in the blessing of God upon his ministry and work, than this humble, unassuming servant of God. But "The humble in due time shall be exalted," and his labors owned and crowned.

There were born to this union two sons and a daughter.

1 MARGARET JANE TELFORD.[5]
2 REV. McMINN D. TELFORD.[5]
3 REV. HERBERT McGEACH TELFORD.[5]

1 MARGARET JANE TELFORD.[5]

1 MARGARET JANE TELFORD[5] was born April 23, 1864. She attended Westminster College, took a course in music, and taught music for a time. She was married to Rev. WILLIAM C. ADAIR, son of Rev. John M. Adair, and brother of Prof. John Calvin Adair of Tarkio College, Missouri, on September 7, 1892, by her father, assisted by Rev. J. M. Adair, Rev. T. Scott and the writer, in the Wurtemburg church, where her

Rev. M. S. Telford.

(Page 105.)

father was pastor at the time. She was a beautiful and accomplished young lady, and well fitted by experience and education for the place she occupies as a pastor's wife.

Rev. W. C. Adair graduated at Westminster College June 19, 1888; was principal of Stone Valley Academy in 1888 and 1889; entered Allegheny Theological Seminary the fall of 1889. The following year he was in Princeton Theological Seminary. The third year he spent at Xenia Seminary, where he graduated May 4, 1892. He was licensed to preach the gospel at Albany, New York, by Albany Presbytery, May 12, 1892. He was ordained and installed pastor of Tuscarara and Concord by Big Spring Presbytery, August 30, 1892. He is a young brother of fine Christian spirit and good attainments, and is doing good work for the Master. The writer has known him from childhood.

To them were born two children:

ANNA RUTH ADAIR,[6] born July, 1893

SARAH HELEN ADAIR,[6] born April 22, 1895.

2 REV. McMINN D. TELFORD.[5]

2 REV. McMINN D. TELFORD[5] was born in Jacksonville, Indiana County, Pennsylvania, February 17, 1867. He was married to Miss MINNIE V. MORRISON, of Wurtemburg, Lawrence County, Pennsylvania, April 17, 1895, by his father, Rev. M. S. Telford.

Rev. M. D. Telford graduated from Westminster College June 24, 1891, and from Allegheny Theological Seminary in May, 1894. He was licensed April 11, 1893, by Conemaugh Presbytery; ordained September 8, 1896, by Sidney Presbytery, and installed over Silver Creek congregation at the same time. He spent one season before this as supply in Kansas. A call was made out for him, but he did not feel justified in accepting it. He has since demitted his charge at Silver Creek, and has accepted a call to Raccoon congregation, New Sheffield, Pennsylvania, and was recently installed there.   Rev. M. D. Telford is a fine penman, and a skilful musician both vocal and instrumental.   He played in and drilled cornet bands when a young man.   He is a ready writer, a good thinker and a good preacher, and that is enough of good to say of any man.

To Rev. and Mrs. Telford was born one child.

GERTRUDE MAY TELFORD,[6] born May 13, 1896, who died
     February 21, 1900.

3 REV. HERBERT McGEACH TELFORD.[5]

3 REV. HERBERT M. TELFORD[5] was born April 1, 1875. He attended Westminster and Muskingum Colleges, graduating at the latter June 25, 1896.   He was licensed to preach April 11, 1898, and ordained September 12, 1899, by Conemaugh Presbytery.   He graduated from Allegheny Seminary May 17, 1899. Since his ordination he has been elected Professor of Greek in Knoxville College, Tennessee.

Surely any father should feel proud of such a family. While brother Telford has sustained a great loss in the death of his excellent wife, and is left lonely, yet he has much to comfort him in his family.   He is pleasantly situated at Homer City, as pastor of the congregation at that place and Crete.   May his bow abide in the strength of the Almighty.

All the family are in the United Presbyterian Church.

6 THOMAS BARR.[4]

6 THOMAS BARR,[4] the last of Uncle Robert Barr's children by his first wife, was born January 25, 1849, in Jackson township, Huntingdon County, Pennsylvania.   He lived with his father on the farm for many years, and then married Miss SANER, a neighbor girl, daughter of John Saner.   They had two children. He and his wife parted, and he is working for the Greenwood

Furnace Company. She is dead. He is an industrious, sober, hard-working man.

Uncle Robert Barr[3] married for his second wife MARY MAGILL, of Huntingdon County, Pennsylvania, a sister of Rev. John A. Magill, and daughter of James Magill, April 23, 1861. She died September 3, 1865, aged forty-three years, three months and eleven days. She was a woman of fine Christian spirit, as were all her father's family, but not a strong woman physically. There was born to this union one child.

MARGARET JANE BARR.[5]

MARGARET JANE BARR[5] was born November 13, 1862, and after her mother's death made her home with her half-sister, Mrs. M. S. Telford. She still lives, and assists her Aunt Kate McMinn in making a home for brother Telford. She never married. She is fine looking, a good Christian girl, and a good housekeeper.

Uncle Robert Barr[3] married for his third wife Mrs. MARY STEWART, widow of William Stewart, on February 28, 1866. She had two daughters living, almost young ladies. There were no children to this union. She died January 11, 1880. She was a member of the Presbyterian Church before marriage, and after marriage joined the United Presbyterian Church with her husband.

IV JANE BARR.[3]

4 Aunt JANE BARR,[3] third daughter of SAMUEL BARR,[2] was born April 17, 1806. She was married to JAMES GRAY April 27, 1837.

Mr. Gray was born in Huntingdon County, Pennsylvania, February 13, 1813, but when a young man removed with his parents to Mercer County, Pennsylvania, where he remained for three years. After this he removed to Ohio, and lived successively in the counties of Coshocton, Putnam, Hardin, and Morrow, where he died at Iberia. His business was farming, and he understood this science very well and made a good living at it. He had during his time fine fruit orchards, and fish ponds where he had his own fish. It was a pleasant place to visit, for they were both very kind, hospitable people, and the latchstring was always out to preachers, and frequently pulled by them. They were worthy members of the United Presbyterian Church. He was a ruling elder in the Leipsic and Kenton congregations for many years. Mr. Gray died of catarrhal fever at the age of sixty-seven, and was buried at Iberia April 5, 1880. His pastor was Rev. J. P. Robb, D. D., who officiated at his funeral, and was a frequent visitor in the home. Mr. Gray never missed a Sabbath at church when it was possible to be present.

His wife died September 5, 1881, of flux. She was seventy-five years of age at her death, and was buried beside her husband, where they rest in peace, having died in the full assurance of faith. They had four children.

   1 LYDIA M. GRAY.[4]
   2 SAMUEL GRAY.[4]
   3 JAMES W. GRAY.[4]
   4 DAVID B. GRAY.[4]

1 LYDIA MARY GRAY.[4]

1 LYDIA MARY GRAY[4] was born March 13, 1838, in Mercer County, Pennsylvania. She was married to Mr. MILES CARSON FREW, son of Robert and Anna (Hamill) Frew, at Leipsic, Ohio. They have no children. They live at present near Loda, Iroquois, County, Illinois. They own their own farm and are comfortably fixed.

Mrs. Anna Barr Telford.

(Page 105.)

2 SAMUEL GRAY.⁴

2 SAMUEL GRAY⁴ was born January 2, 1840, in Mercer County, Pennsylvania. He was in the Civil War. He enlisted in Company G, Eighty-seventh Ohio Regiment, at Leipsic, Putnam County, Ohio, and took part in the battle of Harper's Ferry. This was the only battle he was in, as he was taken prisoner there, and died of camp fever at his father's house, in Putnam County, Ohio, October 28, 1862.

3 JAMES GRAY.⁴

3 JAMES GRAY⁴ was born July 2, 1841, in Mercer County, Pennsylvania, and was married to CHRISTIAN E. REED, near Iberia, Ohio. They are still living, and farm the homestead at Iberia, Ohio. They have worked hard to pay off the other heirs and own the farm unencumbered, which after years of toil they have accomplished.

They have two sons.

1 WILLIAM H. F. GRAY.⁵
2 DAVID R. GRAY.⁵

1 WILLIAM H. F. GRAY.⁵

1 WILLIAM H. F. GRAY⁵ was born at Iberia, Ohio, May 29, 1867. He married Miss ETHEL CRISPIN September 12, 1893. They have no children. They live in their own beautiful home, which they built on one corner of his father's farm, near Iberia railway station, soon after they were married. He is working for the Big Four Railway Company, and is foreman of a section, with fifteen men under him. They are getting along prosperously.

2 DAVID R. GRAY.⁵

2 DAVID R. GRAY⁵ was born at Iberia, Ohio, December 19, 1872. He was married to FLORENCE MAY CALDWELL, by her uncle, Rev. John T. Caldwell, pastor of Iberia United

Presbyterian Church, May 23, 1900. He lives at home and
farms the place.

Mr. James Gray and wife and sons and their wives are all
members of the United Presbyterian Church.

4 DAVID B. GRAY.[4]

4 DAVID B. GRAY[4] was born in Mercer County, Pennsylvania, July 11, 1845. He never married, and died March 3,
1866, at Iberia.

This is one of the quiet, unobstrusive families, never push-
ing themselves into notoriety, but working quietly, and doing
their duty faithfully in the more humble spheres of life. Family
worship is maintained with the utmost regularity morning and
evening in the homes of this family, as well as many other families of this branch of the connection, to the writer's personal
knowledge, and which is true of the connection generally, and
accounts very largely for their integrity as a family.

V SAMUEL BARR.[3]

5 SAMUEL BARR,[3] second son of SAMUEL BARR,[2] was born
in Huntingdon County, Pennsylvania, December 10, 1807.
He was married twice. His first wife's name was JANE McCOR-
MICK,[4] daughter of Polly McCormick, and granddaughter of
David Barr of Center County, Pennsylvania.

To them were born several children, all of whom died
quite young, except one daughter.

MARY BARR.[4]

MARY BARR[4] was born December 14, 1837, in Huntingdon
County, Pennsylvania. She married GEORGE BARR,[4] grandson
of David Barr, Center County, Pennsylvania, April 10, 1856.
They moved to Missouri in 1859, and are living now at DeSoto,
Missouri. (See page 77 for further notice.)

Samuel Barr³ married for his second wife Mrs. HETTY FURY, April 8, 1858. They were married by Rev. Hill of the Presbyterian Church. Mr. Barr died October 23, 1866. Mrs. Barr is still living at Williamsport, Pennsylvania, with her daughter by her first husband, Mrs. Kate (Fury) Irvine. She is in her eighty-fifth year, having been born April 6, 1816.

She was an aunt very highly esteemed; always ready to help in sickness. She was a good housekeeper and a fine cook. She was a lusty woman, but strong and willing. A letter from her a short time ago is highly prized, as it called back many pleasant recollections. She was a member of the United Presbyterian Church of Stone Valley, where she united after her marriage with her husband.

To this union one son was born.

GEORGE M. BARR.⁴

GEORGE M. BARR⁴ was born July 6, 1860, in Stone Valley, Huntingdon County, Pennsylvania. He was married to Miss CARRIE E. CHAPPELL, of Williamsport, Pennsylvania, November 16, 1881, by Rev. M. S. Genve. Mr. Barr is an engineer on the B. & L. E. Railway, and makes his home at Delmar, Delaware. He is a member of the Brotherhood of Locomotive Engineers of the Eastern Shore Division No. 374.

VI JAMES BARR.³

6 JAMES BARR,³ father of the writer of this history, was born October 3, 1809. He lived with his father until after he was of age, and then securing some land, kept bachelor's apartments for a while. He was married to Miss NANCY COOPER BICKETT April 25, 1844. She was born in 1819, on a farm adjoining the old Barr homestead, in Huntingdon County, Pennsylvania. She was the daughter of William and Jennie (Cooper) Bickett, old pioneer settlers in the valley.

William Bickett and his brother Adam Bickett came to this country from the north of Ireland, County Antrim, in 1794. They lost their course and were twenty weeks in crossing the ocean, and almost perished with thirst and hunger. They were of Scotch-Irish descent, and a hardy, sturdy people of good habits and morals.

William Bickett settled in Huntingdon County soon after coming to the State of Pennsylvania. He was married twice. His first wife was a daughter of Duncan McVicker, a government spy among the Indians.

His second wife was Jennie Cooper, born in Mifflin County, Pennsylvania. She lived to the great age (according to her brother's reckoning) of one hundred and three years. The family records were burned when she was a child. She died December 9, 1876. She retained all her faculties until her death. She was a woman who had great faith in God, and had long waited for the home-going. To her were born three children: Robert Bickett, Nancy Cooper Bickett, Samuel Bickett.

They are all dead. Samuel occupied the old Bickett homestead, and died there. Grandfather William Bickett died March 6, 1843, aged seventy-six years.

After the death of my father, mother with the help of the family continued on the farm for five years. But when my only brother died, and I married, and was prosecuting my theological studies with a view to the ministry, and my sisters both married, the farm was sold and mother moved to the fort to live, where she died August 3, 1882, of cholera morbus, after three days of great suffering. She was ten years younger than father. She lived a widow ten years, and died at about the same age as he, in the full assurance of faith.

She was a faithful and devoted wife and mother, kind to the poor, liberal to the church, and beloved by all who knew

Mrs. Nancy C. Barr.
(Page 113.)

Mr. James Barr.
(Page 113.)

her. She left a legacy of three hundred dollars to the church, to be placed on interest, to continue her subscription so long as there was a United Presbyterian congregation in that place ; so that her good deeds live after her.

Father died suddenly and unexpectedly on March 31, 1872, in his sixty-fourth year. He retired quite as well as usual and never awoke. Mother noticed him holding his breath, and thinking he was holding it too long, undertook to arouse him ; but not succeeding, called for my brother, who slept in an adjoining room. They raised him up, but he was gone. He had complained of his heart losing a beat occasionally, but nothing was thought of it until after his death. He died of heart failure. Few get out of this world so easily.

My father was a very industrious man, and a very successful farmer. He cleared most of his own land, and erected almost all of his own buildings. This was a difficult task, as the land was heavily timbered. He was said to own one of the best farms in the valley.

He was a ruling elder in the United Presbyterian Church, near McAlevy's Fort, for perhaps thirty years. He was an able counsellor, and always a friend of the pastor. He never criticised his pastor before his family, nor would he suffer others to do so. The pastor, Rev. J. M. Adair, who for fourteen years of his pastorate had been associated with him in the session, remarked at his funeral with considerable emotion, "I have lost one of my best friends and safest counsellors." He was never known to be absent from church without a reason that he could offer to God. He never, under any circumstances, neglected family worship morning and evening. The mid-week prayer-meeting was never neglected either. The week before he died, when the roads were at their worst, he rode on horseback across Stone Mountain to Lewiston on business, and returned the same day, making forty miles. After eating his supper he took another horse and rode two miles to prayer-meeting. This was characteristic of the man. He always made his religion his first duty. And because he looked after God's business, God looked after his, and he prospered in material things as his soul prospered. It would be a shame for children, with such an example set before them, and raised in such a religious atmosphere, not to be religious. Hence we have nothing whereof we can boast before God, "for when we have done all, we can only say we are unprofitable servants; we have done that which was our duty to do."

There were born to them eight children:

1 JANE COOPER BARR,[4] born April 27, 1845, and died of diphtheria April 12, 1860.

2 SAMUEL EASTON BARR,[4] born March 24, 1847, and died September 11, 1851.

3 ELIZABETH BARR,[4] born May 16, 1849, died June 14, 1850.

4 WILLIAM BICKETT BARR.[4]

5 ANNA MARY BARR.[4]

6 JAMES ANDERSON BARR.[4]

7 LAURA AGNES BARR.[4]

8 Infant, stillborn.

4 REV. WILLIAM BICKETT BARR.[4]

4 REV. WILLIAM BICKETT BARR[4] was born November 11, 1851, near McAlevy's Fort, Pennsylvania.

[I would prefer that another's pen might trace this section of our history. Modesty teaches me that I should not deviate from the practice of the use of the third person of the pronoun in inditing the record of my own life.]

He lived on the farm and attended the district schools until he was fifteen years old; he then entered the select school afterward organized as Stone Valley Academy, for four years.

Mrs. Mary Alice Barr.

(Page 120.)

He entered Westminster College, New Wilmington, Pennsylvania, in 1870, and graduated from the same institution in June, 1875; attended the Theological Seminary at Allegheny, Pennsylvania, and Xenia, Ohio, graduating from the former in April, 1878.

He was licensed to preach the gospel by Big Spring Presbytery, in April, 1878, and ordained and installed by Butler Presbytery June 10, 1879, as pastor of Springfield United Presbyterian congregation. This call he accepted in January, on condition that he be permitted to start a mission church at Pine Grove, six miles distant (now known as Grove City). In March, 1879, he began work at Pine Grove, and organized it by direction of Presbytery September 1, 1879, with thirty-one members. He was installed pastor over this congregation in connection with Springfield, August 6, 1880. It grew rapidly, and had the elements of a successful church. During this settlement he partially rebuilt, changed, and beautified the church building at Springfield; and built a new church at Pine Grove in 1882, costing almost six thousand dollars, which would seat five hundred people.

He resigned this charge in May, 1885, to accept a unanimous call from the New Brighton congregation, leaving one hundred and forty-five members in each congregation. They then became two separate charges. He began the work at New Brighton in May, 1885, and was installed July 14, 1885, by Beaver Valley Presbytery. During this pastorate he built a new church at New Brighton, costing fifteen thousand dollars; built a new church for mission purposes in Fallston, on the other side of the river, under the direction of the New Brighton congregation. He was also made chairman of the building committee to erect a new church at Ellwood City, under the direction of Beaver Valley Presbytery, in the summer of 1891, costing twenty-eight hundred dollars, which was dedicated without debt, although there was no congregation there at the time, and the town was just starting. He resigned the New Brighton church October 1, 1891, to accept a very hearty call from First United Presbyterian Church, Xenia, Ohio, leaving the church with three hundred and fifteen members, and closing one of the most successful six years' work of his life.

He entered upon the work at Xenia in November, 1891, and resigned December 17, 1892, to enter upon evangelistic and missionary work, having been strongly urged to do so, and receiving many calls from brethren for that kind of work. It was a kind of work of which he had made a special study, and in which he found much pleasure during all the years of his ministry.

After holding meetings in Pennsylvania, Ohio, and Michigan, he received an invitation to take charge of Dr. Irvine's congregation, at Albany, Oregon, for a few months, he being laid aside with inflammatory rheumatism. This he accepted, and left his home at New Brighton March 4, 1893, for Oregon, where he remained for six months, holding meetings in Portland, Albany, Willamette, and Shedds, Oregon; and Seattle, Washington. Over one hundred were added to the churches that spring.

On September 5th he left for California, accompanied by his wife. After holding meetings in a few places in California, he was invited to take charge of the First Los Angeles congregation, which had just split, the pastor having gone out of it and formed the second church. The work was so broken up, the people were so discouraged, and the field so occupied with other large, flourishing churches, that it looked like a hopeless undertaking to try to build up the congregation again. But having received an urgent request from the congregation, and also from the Presbytery, to undertake the work, he consented to remain for the winter and do what he could for them. He remained there a year and nine months, and during that time under the divine blessing the church increased from forty-two to ninety-eight members, and the work was entirely reorganized. The Chinese mission, which had been under the care of Dr. Nevin, and was disbanded by him because he felt he could no longer carry on the work, was reorganized and started in a new building, which was bought by the Chinese boys and modernized. He baptized three Chinese from heathenism before leaving, also administered the Lord's Supper to them. This mission has doubled since it was reorganized. He endeavored to put the congregation into shape to call a pastor permanently, as they had from their organization been served by stated supplies. This they did after he left, and have continued to flourish.

He decided to return East, and closed his work July 1, 1895. On his return East he preached a few places along the way. Stopping over at Chicago for a few days, he occupied the Third United Presbyterian Church pulpit, which was vacant, and from which he afterward received a very urgent call, which he declined, having begun work at Middletown, Ohio.

This was a new church just started by the Presbytery of First Ohio, which, with the aid of the young people's societies of the presbytery, had erected a neat church building in a suitable location. An application from presbytery was awaiting him on his return East, to take hold of this field. He decided to remain for the winter as supply, and do what he could for them and test the field. Having received forty-seven members during the winter, he consented to a call being made, which was accepted at the June meeting of presbytery, 1896. He was installed over Middletown church September, 1896. Here he remained until December 1, 1898, when he resigned to accept a unanimous call to the First United Presbyterian Church, Hoboken, New Jersey, where he is at present enjoying the

work. During his stay at Middletown the debt was reduced
from two thousand to four hundred dollars, many improvements made about the church, the congregation increased from
eleven to eighty members, and all the departments of work well
organized. Of those received into the church by profession,
almost all were baptised, and very few of the members were
raised in the United Presbyterian faith. But a more loyal little
church it would be difficult to find.

He has nothing to say of himself in all that has been
accomplished, but points to Him who giveth the increase and
says, "See what God hath wrought;" to whom be all the glory.

Rev. Barr has always taken an active part in the reform
movements of the day. He has voted the Prohibition ticket
since 1879, and so is of age as a prohibition voter; and until he
sees some reason to change, will continue to vote this ticket.
He was nominated for Congress in 1884 by Mercer County,
Pennsylvania, a strong temperance county. May God in his
time give victory to the right.

Rev. Barr was married twice. His first marriage was to
Miss MARY ALICE CUMMINS, daughter of Sterrett and Agnes
(McNitt) Cummins, of Stone Valley, Huntingdon County,
Pennsylvania, by Rev. John M. Adair, assisted by Rev. Robert
W. Kidd, June 22, 1876. She was born May 24, 1853. They
were brought up in the same church, went to the same academy,
and knew each other from childhood.

Mrs. Barr's family deserves more than passing notice, as
two of the writer's sisters and some of his cousins married into
this connection.

Her father and mother were full cousins, her paternal
grandfather, Mr. Robert Cummins, having married a sister of
her maternal grandmother, whose names were Mary and Nancy
Sterrett, daughters of David and Elizabeth (Hannah) Sterrett.
Her Grandfather Cummins's parents, Samuel and Sallie (Semple)

Mr. Sterret Cummins.

(Page 121.)

Cummins, came from the north of Ireland, to Lancaster, Pennsylvania, at an early day. Of them we know but little.

Mr. Robert Cummins was a highly esteemed citizen. His was one of the chief families of the United Presbyterian Church of that valley, which is now one hundred years old. Mr. Cummins gave the ground for the church, found the lumber (as he had two saw-mills), hauled the stone, found the carpenters and masons, and boarded them while the church was being built. The congregation sometimes met in his barn for service, before they had a church building. He was one of the financial pillars of the church until his death. He raised a large, intelligent and highly respected family of seven sons and four daughters, the eldest of whom, Cyrus Cummins, was a minister of the gospel. This large family married, and for the most part lived and brought up their families in that valley, and became members of that church.

Sterrett Cummins, was born April 24, 1829, near McAlevy's Fort, Pennsylvania. He married Agnes McNitt March 4, 1852. She was born January 24, 1830, in Mifflin County, Pennsylvania. They lived and raised their large family on a farm adjoining the old Cummins homestead, and originally a part of it. Father and mother Cummins were a most amiable, social and entertaining couple. Their hospitality was widely known. Father Cummins was a well informed man on questions of public and religious interest. He had an excellent mind, was an independent thinker, an able counsellor and above the average of farmers in business sagacity and intellectual breadth. He owned three farms under good state of cultivation, and could make money in any kind of times. He was liberal to the church and a most regular and faithful attendant upon all of its services, and for a number of years a ruling elder. He died suddenly of paralysis, at his home, December 17, 1894.

Mother Cummins was a model mother and housekeeper, a kind and accommodating neighbor, a friend to every one. She carefully trained her family of girls, industriously, socially and religiously; so that they could run a farm as well as a house, and make a bargain as well as sew a garment. I know I have not said too much, as those who knew the family will bear me out. It is said, "A wise rule in choosing a wife, to be happy, is to choose a good mother and marry one of her daughters." Mother Cummins died of paralysis, at her home, November 25, 1888. She went out to feed the poultry in the morning, and fell in the meadow near the house. There being no one at home at the time, she lay out all day. There was a light snow on the ground. She was still breathing when they found her, after a long search, but she never spoke, and died a few hours after being taken into the house. Thus ended a beautiful and useful life.

Mrs. Barr went with her husband to the Theological Seminary at Allegheny the last two years of his course. She was a most excellent woman, possessed of many amiable qualities and much natural ability. She had a most excellent mind, and made a helpful minister's wife. She was under size and never very robust, but seldom ever sick in bed. She held many offices in the Presbyterial Ladies' Missionary Society, and was three times elected to the general Ladies' Missionary Society of the United States. She made friends everywhere she went, and held them to her.

She accompanied her husband to the coast, thinking the trip might benefit her health, as she had been suffering from asthmatic trouble, precipitated by the lagrippe when at Xenia, Ohio. She had enjoyed the trip and improved in health up to the time she reached LosAngeles, California, when her trouble returned and she became suddenly worse, and died of heart failure, through exhaustion from excessive coughing, and loss of

Mrs. Agnes Cummins.

(Page 121.)

appetite, December 31, 1893, at Redlands, California, and was
buried in Evergreen Cemetery, at Los Angeles.

This was a terrible blow to her husband, as well as
her people, and sadly marred the trip. How quickly our joy
is turned to mourning. Her life was beautiful, and she seemed
to be taken away in the midst of her usefulness. It is a great
mystery to us often why the worthless are spared to be a pest
to society and the good and useful are cut down in the midst of
their usefulness. Her husband bowed humbly to the will of
Providence, knowing that He doeth all things well. He had the
sympathy and help of many willing hands to lay her peacefully
to rest. "Blessed are the dead that die in the Lord; they do
rest from their labors, and their works do follow them."

To this union there was no issue.

After his first wife's death, being strongly urged to continue
the work which had been so auspiciously begun at Los Angeles,
he decided to stay for a year; but remained in all about a year
and nine months. During his stay he met Miss AGNES HARRIS,
daughter of John P. and Margaret (Rutherford) Harris, of
Harrisville, West Virginia, who came to California in April, 1894,
to teach school and enjoy a change of climate for a year. She
had taught school for nine years before coming to California.
At the close of their work they were united in marriage on June
18, 1895, at Riverside, by Rev. A. W. Jamison, then of
Wildomar. After visiting a number of places of interest along
the coast, they returned East, stopping at Salt Lake City,
Denver, Manitou Springs, Pike's Peak, Omaha and Chicago,
arriving at the bride's home in West Virginia, July 31, 1895.
After visiting friends they entered upon the work at Middletown.

As to Mrs. Barr's ancestors, her paternal great-grandfather
was John Harris, who was born in Ireland. He came to this
country, settling in New Jersey, where he married Mrs. Miller
(*nee* Plunimer). They moved to Harrison County, Virginia,

(now West Virginia) in 1795, where he died of consumption. They had seven children.

John, the second son, married Agnes Maley, daughter of Mr. and Mrs. Lawrence Maley, in 1810. (Mrs. Lawrence Maley was a Harper.) He came to Wood County, Virginia, in 1809. She died in 1860, and Mr. Harris died in 1863. The new county of Ritchie, West Virginia, was organized in his house. Harrisville, the county seat, is named for the family. Also Harrisburg, Pennsylvania, is said to have been named for the connection. He was the first sheriff of Ritchie County, and for many years the justice of the peace, and very prominent in the county. To them were born eight children: Mary, Thomas, Hannah, James, Jane, John P., Ann and Margaret.

John Plunimer Harris, the father of Mrs. Barr, was born February 29, 1820, and hence he only had a birthday every four years. He died of an abscess of the liver, November 13, 1886. He was a modest, retiring man, but highly esteemed in the community, and from the time he was a young man he was never without a public office. He was a very intelligent man, a great reader, and a man whose integrity was never called into question.

His brother, Gen. T. M. Harris, M. D., was a practicing physician in Ritchie County for many years, and gained great distinction in the Civil War. He recruited and organized the Tenth Virginia Regiment. He was made Lieutenant Colonel in December, 1861, and advanced to First Brigadier-General of First Division, under General Thoburn. He was appointed Brigadier-General by President Lincoln March 29, 1865. He was the last Brigadier-General Lincoln appointed. He participated actively until the close of the war. He was in several battles, and had his horse shot from under him several times, but was never shot himself. He silenced the last guns at Appomattox. He hindered General Gordon's escape. He was

Mrs. Agnes Harris Barr.

(Page 123.)

in command of the Freedmen's Bureau until December 25, 1865. He was mustered out April 30, 1866. He was a member of the commission appointed by the government to try the conspirators against Lincoln. He has published the full account of that trial in a very interesting volume, and also another volume on Catholicism. He is a man of fine intellect, an interesting conversationalist, and a Christian gentleman of high standing. He is a ruling elder in the Cairo United Presbyterian Church. He is in his eighty-seventh year, and lives at Harrisville, West Virginia.

Mrs. Barr's maternal grandparents were Richard and Eleanor (Wauless) Rutherford, who were married at Leith, Scotland, June 22, 1819. He was born in September, 1791, and died April 7, 1880. She was born March 23, 1797, and died June 5, 1879. They had ten children: Mary, Ellen, Ann, George, Archibald, Susannah, Margaret, Isabella, Katherine, and Jane.

Margaret, the mother of Mrs. Barr, was born October 17, 1832, and died suddenly of heart failure, in New York City, on her way to the home of Mrs. Barr for New Years dinner from her other daughter's, Mrs. Rev. E. S. Littell's, January 1, 1900. She was married to Mr. Harris January 8, 1861.

She was a woman of meek and quiet spirit, an estimable Christian lady, and raised her large family in the fear of the Lord. As a mother she was kind, industrious, and forgiving, careful in rebuking wrong-doing, and encouraging and teaching right principles, and always setting an example of piety and nobleness. She was peaceful in her life, and her death was without pain. Instead of sitting down at our table, she was called to celebrate her New Year at the banqueting table of God in her Father's house above, with husband and friends who had preceded her. She was translated from the banks of the beautiful Hudson River to the banks of the crystal sea;

and from the Empire City to walk the golden streets of the capital city of God.

She was buried beside her husband, at Harrisville, on January 4, 1900.

To them were born seven children, all of whom are living but the eldest: James, Richard R., Agnes Eleanor, Mary, John Lawrence, Annabelle, and Thomas George.

James died of consumption, at home, February 8, 1887.

Richard Rutherford occupies the homestead, at Harrisville, West Virginia.

Mary is the wife of Rev. E. S. Littell, formerly of New York city, now of Zelienople, Pennsylvania.

John Lawrence lives at Weston, West Virginia.

Annabelle at present is matron of the Boys' Home, at Knoxville College, Knoxville, Tennessee.

Thomas George is attending the Medical Department of Pennsylvania University at Philadelphia, Pennsylvania.

Mrs. Barr attended Muskingum College at New Concord, Ohio, from 1884 to 1886. She is a woman of good judgment and a good mind, a companionable and loving wife, filling her sphere in the home and the church with great acceptance.

To them were born three children.

EDWARD HARRIS BARR,[5] born at Middletown, Ohio, March 23, 1896.

Infant, stillborn, October 8, 1897.

JAMES CLARK BARR,[6] born October 27, 1898, at Middletown, Ohio; died at Hoboken, New Jersey, of pneumonia, December 11, 1899.

He was a bright, promising child, and his loss was a trying one. They were comforted in their boys, but their hopes were soon blasted. The Lord had need of him. But the experience was valuable to them, as it has prepared them to enter into the feelings of those who have met with a similar loss.

Each life has its Gethsemanes and its transfigurations; its Beulahs and its Baca Valleys; its sunshine and its shadows; and to be able to say "Thy will be done," in the one as in the other, is a triumph of faith.

5 ANNA M. BARR.[4]

5 ANNA M. BARR[4] was born September 20, 1853. She attended Westminster College in 1871-72. She was married to JOHN C. CUMMINS, son of Samuel and Catherine (Smith) Cummins, by Rev. John M. Adair, December 24, 1874.

After their marriage they farmed the homestead for one year. My sister then bought a farm on the East Branch, adjoining my other sister's home. Mr. Cummins had for some time expressed a preference for medicine, and to this end completed the full course at the Medical University of Baltimore, graduating there in 1882. They then rented the farm and bought a home in the fort, where he practiced for some time successfully. He proved unfaithful to his wife, and she secured a divorce from the courts, after which he left the community and went West. This hastened the death of his wife, who, after months of suffering from organic heart trouble, which turned to dropsy of a violent type, found rest in death. She died at the home of her sister Laura, June 21, 1890.

She was a Sabbath-school teacher, an earnest worker in the Woman's Christian Temperance Union, and a faithful member and liberal supporter of the church in which she had been raised. Before her death she bequeathed one hundred and fifty dollars to Foreign Missions, the same amount each to Home Mission and Church Extension Boards. She also donated three hundred dollars to the church in selling her home for a church parsonage. She was a true child of God, and loved his church and work.

6 JAMES A. BARR.[4]

6 James A. Barr[4] was born October 20, 1855, and died of pneumonia, February 6, 1874, after six days' illness. For some time before his death he attended to the duty of family worship. He was a member of the church, and librarian of the Sabbath-school at the time of his death, and never neglected to attend church and Sabbath-school. Before his death he left a legacy of one thousand dollars, to be put on interest for the benefit of the Sabbath-school library. Special provision has been made in the church for the library, which bears his name. And it is, perhaps, one of the largest and best libraries of any congregation in the body to-day. It has been of incalculable value to the community, where there is an academy on the grounds adjacent to the church, and largely under the control of the church. Surely the Lord prompted the idea. Would that we had more such legacies. He was not married.

7 LAURA AGNES BARR.[4]

7 Laura Agnes Barr[4] was born February 22, 1857, and was married to Robert C. Wilson, son of John A. and Nancy (Cummins) Wilson, by Rev. John M. Adair, January 2, 1879. Mr. Wilson was our nearest neighbor, and bought the homestead in 1878. After my sister's marriage, they farmed the homestead for one year, and then bought a farm of two hundred and fifty acres, on the East Branch.

Mr. Wilson is an elder of the United Presbyterian Church, in which he was raised. He is a liberal supporter of the church, and the family never miss a service without good cause.

To them were born four children.

John Vernon Wilson[5] was born October 3, 1879, and died February 26, 1892. His death was peculiarly sad. He was kicked on the head by one of the horses in play, while he was leading it to water. An artery was severed and his skull crushed, from which he died in a few hours, never regaining consciousness. He was in the thirteenth year of his age. He was a member of the church, and had led the young people's prayer-meeting the Sabbath previous to his death. He was a bright, promising boy, and a good worker. His death was a severe blow to the family.

JAMES BARR WILSON[5] was born November 15, 1881. He lives at home and is a member of the church.

WILLIAM FRANK WILSON[5] was born August 6, 1886.

MARY ELEANOR WILSON[5] was born November 13, 1891. She was able to read in the newspaper when she was five years of age. She is a studious girl.

All of the family are dead but Laura and the writer. As the writer looks about, and memories of the past crowd in upon him, feelings of loneliness steal over him. But the servant who frequently consults his time-piece, and longs for the sunset, is unworthy of his master, and bears but little love for his master's work, or interest in his master's glory. "Be ye not weary in well doing; for in due time ye shall reap, if ye faint not." The rest that remaineth for the people of God will be all the more glorious after a life of service.

This closes the history of my father's family; a history strewn with early graves and many tears, but tears that glisten in the light of the hope of a glorious reunion on the other shore.

VII GABRIEL BARR.[8]

7 Uncle GABRIEL BARR[8] was born October 2, 1811. He was married to Miss LILLY ANN SCOTT March 16, 1836. She was born April 1, 1818, and died of consumption August 26, 1866, at Fountain Green, Hancock County, Illinois.

Uncle Gabriel after he was married lived for a number of years in sight of the old homestead. He ran the saw-mill and tannery business, and for a time was very successful. He and his family moved from Huntingdon County, Pennsylvania, to Lee County, Iowa, in the fall of 1854. He farmed in the west. He owned his own farm of one hundred and sixty acres. He raised great crops of corn and wheat, but had very bad luck with his stock. He lost twenty-five head of horses in eleven years, and his cattle died with "black tongue," and his hogs with the cholera. The war broke out, and the two oldest boys enlisted in the army. He sold out and moved to Fountain Green in the fall of 1865, where he spent the remainder of his days. He died March 23, 1877, of stomach trouble, in his sixty-sixth year. Aunt died in her forty-eighth year. They had ten children, four sons and six daughters.

1 SAMUEL BARR.[4]
2 JAMES BARR.[4]
3 HANNAH BARR.[4]
4 SARAH ELIZABETH BARR.[4]
5 WILHELMINA SCOTT BARR.[4]
6 FRANCIS ANN BARR.[4]
7 MARY EMELINE BARR.[4]
8 LILLIE HAMILTON BARR.[4]
9 EDWARD CARL BARR.[4]
10 ALBERT LEACH BARR.[4]

1 SAMUEL BARR.[4]

1 SAMUEL BARR[4] was born January 10, 1838, in Huntingdon County, Pennsylvania. He went to college in Washington, Iowa. He was a very fine penman, and taught penmanship for a while. He was very handy with tools, and decided to become an architect. He went to Fort Madison and worked at his trade one year, when the Civil War broke out, and he came home and enlisted in the army in 1861. There was much sadness in the home when he made known his intentions. The probability was that they would never see him again.

Mr. Gabriel Barr.

(Page 129.)

He was First Sergeant of Company B, Third Iowa Cavalry, and in 1863 was promoted to the office of Captain of the same company. In 1864 he was wounded and taken to the hospital at Kansas City, Missouri, and there took pneumonia and soon after died. He was shot through the thigh, and had his limb amputated. He knew he was going to die, and made all arrangements with one of his comrades to be sent home. He died November 28, 1864. His comrade accompanied his remains, and he was buried with the honors of war. He was a brave man, and a good soldier. His life was a truly noble one, as his letters in possession of his sister Mary show. His letter in answer to one from Mr. A. B. McCord of his company, tells of what kind of stuff he was made. It was written while he was in bed.

LETTER OF CAPTAIN SAMUEL BARR.

"*To the Boys of Company B, and General:*

"I am flat on my back at present from the effects of the amputation of my left leg. I suppose you will all naturally think that I am about played, so far as soldiering is concerned. I have not come to that conclusion. I feel as well to-day as I ever did in my life, only I am weak. All I want is time and rest, and a wooden leg; then I will be with you again.

"I never enjoyed a trip better in my life, than the last, until the time of my wound.

"Boys, you must give them Cain until I get well, and I will be with you.

"I must close, for there is a young girl getting my supper for me.

"I am your friend,
Sam Barr."

Poor fellow, his soldiering was done. He gave his life for his country.

2 JAMES BARR.[4]

2 JAMES BARR[4] stayed at home and helped his father on the farm. He was a great singer and violinist, and found much enjoyment in it. He enlisted in the Union Army in 1862 in the same company (B) as his brother. In 1864 he was shot through the breast, and died. He fills an unknown grave. One of his comrades, who was with him when he was shot, said it was one of the hardest things he ever did to leave him behind. He was the boss cook for the company, and a noble soldier. He was born August 21, 1839, and died January 4, 1865.

Mr. P. M. Mathews, of Warren, Iowa, who was a comrade of James, and with him when he was shot, writes:

"We started from Memphis, Tennessee, about the 18th of December, 1864, on a cavalry raid commanded by General Griesson with twenty-five hundred men. On January 6, 1865, we camped at Mechanicsburg, and started early on the morning of the 7th for Vicksburg. When we had gone two or three miles, we stopped at a pond by the roadside to water our horses, and the rebels commenced firing upon us. Our company was ordered to drive them back, while the rest of the command continued to water the horses. Our company was formed between the pond and the enemy.

"We were firing briskly at long range, when James was shot through the stomach. I was on his left side and John Merritt was on his right side. We caught him, and I held him on the horse and Merritt led the horse away. We took him about one-fourth of a mile to a house, and the doctor (Maxwell, of Keokuk) removed the ball, which was lodged under the skin, near the spinal column. The lady of the house said her husband was a physician, and promised to take care of him. We put him in bed and undressed him, when the rebels drove us from the house, the rest of the command having gone on. The surgeon said he could not live more than a day or so. Not being able to take him along he was left in the hands of the enemy, and that is the last known of him."

He may have died there, or been killed outright by the rebels. It was a very sad affliction to the family, but he died in a good cause and with his face to the foe, and fills an honorable but unknown grave.

3 HANNAH BARR.[4]

3 HANNAH BARR[4] was born October 25, 1842, and died October 23, 1862. She died of consumption. She went to college for a while, but when her health failed, she came home. She spent the last few years of her life making embroidery and laces, which are admired by all who see them.

4 SARAH ELIZABETH BARR.[4]

4 SARAH E. BARR[4] was born July 21, 1845. She was a milliner by trade, but it was too confining, and she took consumption and died March 25, 1871.

5 WILHELMINA SCOTT BARR.[4]

5 WILHELMINA SCOTT BARR[4] was born January 9, 1848. She was a teacher for some years in Knoxville College, Knoxville, Tennessee, beginning 1877, and making her home with Rev. S. B. Reed, D. D., who was president at the time. She was married to Mr. J. S. FOWLER, of Belmont, New York, by Rev. S. B. Reed, D. D., assisted by Rev. J. S. McCullough, D. D., on July 24, 1879.

Mr. Fowler had been principal of the city schools before their marriage. They both taught in the college for two years, resigning in June, 1881. He was that same year elected principal of the Chattanooga schools, which position he held for four years, at a salary of one hundred and twenty-five dollars a month. They moved from Chattanooga to the side of Lookout Mountain, four miles from Chattanooga, on the edge of Georgia.

They lived there till January, 1891, when Mr. Fowler became secretary of the Northwestern Investment Company. They then moved back to Chattanooga. After a while they moved for the health of the children to Albion View, on Walder's Ridge, where in 1883 they bought a farm of sixty-five acres, set with eight hundred apple trees that never fail to bear.

They are now in Menlo, Georgia, the great fruit belt. They own one hundred and seventy-nine acres of land there. They have five thousand peach trees which are beginning to bear. They had six acres in strawberries this season (1900). Last winter they taught the Pine Grove school, the eldest daughter assisting. They had over ninety pupils.

Mr. and Mrs. Fowler and the two eldest children are members of the Presbyterian Church, and have charge of a union Sabbath-school.

The following children were born to them:

Infant, born July 6, 1880, which only lived a few minutes; born at Knoxville, Tennessee.

Mary Minerva Fowler[6] was also born at Knoxville, November 24, 1881. She is attending Chattanooga Normal University, at Hill City, Tennessee. She will graduate next year. She learns readily and is a very promising girl.

Bessie Fowler[6] was born August 10, 1884, and died July 6, 1885, on the side of Lookout Mountain.

Charles Gilbert Fowler[6] was born in January, 1886, on the side of Lookout Mountain, Walker County, Georgia. He was in the tenth grammar grade school last year, and will graduate at that school next year.

Flossie Fowler[5] was born on Lookout Mountain August 4, 1887, and died January 27, 1888, at the same place.

James Garfield Fowler[5] was born January 1, 1889, on Lookout Mountain. He is attending school at home.

HARRY FOWLER[5] was born in Chattanooga May 11, 1891, and died at Albion View, Tennessee, July 25, 1892.

WILHELMINA FOWLER[5] was born June 29, 1893, at Albion View, Tennessee. She has been at school two months, and reads in third reader and is a good little singer.

They have four living of the eight children. They have been passing through the deep waters of affliction as well as others.

6 FRANCIS ANN BARR.[4]

6 FRANCIS ANN BARR[4] was born May 21, 1850, and died in 1851.

7 MARY EMELINE BARR.[4]

7 MARY EMELINE BARR[4] was born February 23, 1853. She married Mr. WILLIAM LENIX December 14, 1871. He was born in Lancaster County, Pennsylvania, in July, 1843, and came west with his father to Illinois. His parents were born in Lancaster County, Pennsylvania. His mother's maiden name was Elizabeth Allbright. They are of Presbyterian stock back several generations. Mr. Lenix has for years followed shipping cattle, hogs and grain to Chicago as a business, and has done well at it. He owns and conducts a large farm near Webster, Hancock County, Illinois, where they now live. He has retired from business, except to oversee the men on the farm. They have two children living—both boys, and one dead.

BERNARD VANE LENIX[5] was born April 24, 1879. He attended Carthage High School and is a good scholar. He married EMILY ELLEN ERVIN May 2, 1896, and lives on a farm about a mile from his father's home. They have one child.

MARY FOSTER LENIX,[6] born June 4, 1900, the first and only great-grandchild thus far of Gabriel Barr.

EDGAR SCOTT LENIX[5] was born February 16, 1873, and died when one month old.

ALBERT EARL LENIX[5] the youngest son, was born May 16,
1882, and is studying to be a lawyer, and promises to
make a good one.

Mrs. Lenix does a great deal of nursing and caring for the
sick people, and has become very proficient at it, getting much
praise from the physicians. She takes a very active part in
Church work, and is also an active member of the Ladies
Missionary Society. They celebrated the twenty-eighth anniver-
sary of their marriage April 5, 1900, and received some handsome presents and enjoyed a very pleasant time.

8 LILLY HAMILTON BARR.[4]

8 LILLY HAMILTON BARR[4] was born May 21, 1855, and
died when she was sixteen years old. She was preparing herself for a teacher, and broke down with hard study and died.
Two days before she died, she disposed of all her little things,
and told them not to grieve over her, for she was going home.
She died June 11, 1872.

9 EDWARD CARL BARR.[4]

9 EDWARD C. BARR[4] was born September 25, 1858. He
was a natural-born mathematician. He went to college at
Carthage, Illinois. He is a veterinary surgeon. He married
ORPHA E. RUSSELL March 30, 1882, and moved to Waverly,
Kansas. He has been practicing his profession for several years,
and has made quite a success of it. They have five boys.

ALBERT CLYDE BARR,[5] born May 27, 1883.

EARL FOWLER BARR,[5] born February 22, 1886.

ORA RUSSELL BARR,[5] born August 3, 1889.

ROY OLIVE BARR,[5] born April 5, 1891, and died July
10, 1892.

WYNN SCOTT BARR,[5] born September 6, 1892.

10 ALBERT LEACH BARR.[4]

10 ALBERT L. BARR,[4] the youngest of the family, was born October 31, 1861. He married Miss ETTA WHITE November 7, 1894, and lives on a farm near his wife's father. He feeds several car loads of cattle and hogs every year, and ships them to Chicago. He is doing well at it. They have two children living. The eldest was born October 14, 1895, and died October 15, 1895.

ZOLA GLADYS BARR[5] was born January 13, 1897.

ALBERT MARION BARR[5] was born October 1, 1898.

Mr. Albert Barr has been tax collector and assessor for several years, and prominent in the community.

This closes Uncle Gabriel's family—a large, well-to-do family; an honor to their parents and to the connection. They are connected with Presbyterian or United Presbyterian churches, and active workers in the same.

VIII MARGARET BARR.[3]

8 MARGARET BARR[3] was born July 25, 1813, in Huntingdon County, Pennsylvania. She was married to SAMUEL EVERHART BARR, son of Samuel and Susan (Everhart) Barr, June 2, 1836. He was born May 2, 1813, in Center County, Pennsylvania, near Boalsburg. His parents were born in Center County also. His father died in 1818, and his mother married John Sparr and raised a second family.

Aunt Margaret married her full cousin. This was not according to the conservative notions of her people on that question, so she and her husband moved to Iowa, when that was a very new country, where she died December 4, 1847, in Van Buren County, two weeks after her son Samuel was born. To this union were born the following children.

1 Mary Jane Barr.[4]

2 Twin boys born November 30, 1838, died November 31, 1838.

3 Susan Lydia Barr.[4]

4 Sarah Thompson Barr,[4] born September 3, 1841, died September 11, 1845.

5 Elizabeth Reed Barr.[4]

6 Margaret Ann Barr.[4]

7 Samuel McCormick Barr.[4]

1 MARY JANE BARR.[4]

1 Mary Jane Barr[4] was born August 29, 1837, in Center County, Pennsylvania. She died in Van Buren County, Iowa, April 8, 1849.

3 SUSAN LYDIA BARR.[4]

3 Susan Lydia Barr[4] was born November 21, 1839, and was married to Louis Prabzman in Iowa, in 1859. She is dead. The date of her death is unknown. To them were born four children. The two oldest are dead.

Louis Prabzman, Jr.,[5] was born June 30, 1870. He is now living in Dawson City, Alaska.

Eva Prabzman[5] was born in 1875. She is now living in Portland, Oregon.

5 ELIZABETH REED BARR.[4]

5 Elizabeth Reed Barr[4] was born March 28, 1843. She was married to Jeremiah Smith in 1861. She is the mother of four living children.

Edward Smith,[5] born in 1862.

William Grant Smith,[5] born in 1868.

Minnie Smith,[5] born in 1869.

The name of the last child is not known. The family live in California, but their address is not known to the writer.

Mr. Samuel M. Barr.

(Page 139.)

6 MARGARET ANN BARR.[4]

6 MARGARET ANN BARR[4] was born August 30, 1844. She married LYMAN CHITTENDEN in April, 1861. She died in Portland, Oregon, August 2, 1861.

7 SAMUEL McCORMICK BARR.[4]

7 SAMUEL M. BARR,[4] was born April 2, 1847. He married SELINA BARKER January 1, 1875. He came to Oregon with the family April 12, 1859, and was married in Portland.

Mr. Barr worked in the mines of California for a few years when a young man, and got a start in business. He is a man of good business ability, and never found it any trouble to make money. He owned the Barr Hotel, a large four-story building—one of the largest in the city —on the corner of Sixth and Glison Streets, which he sold recently, besides other property in Portland. He is a man of good habits, and himself and family attend the Presbyterian Church of Portland. He is a Republican in politics.

They have been spending their winters in Los Angeles, on account of the children, one of whom is delicate. To them were born four children, two boys and two girls.

GRACE SELINA BARR[5] was born in 1881.

ELSIE SUSAN BARR[5] was born in 1883.

HARRY GRANT BARR[5] was born in 1885.

GEORGE EARL BARR[5] was born in 1887.

The children are all bright and studious. Elsie has carried off some important prizes in the Marlborough School, Los Angeles, the last two years. Harry was with his father the past summer at Cape Nome, Alaska, and is a good little worker. This is one of the quiet, orderly homes where it is a pleasure to visit, as the writer knows from experience.

Mr. Samuel E. Barr[8] married for his second wife Miss MARGARET JANE WATTERMAN. They were married on June

11, 1849, in Van Buren County, Iowa. She was born June 11, 1827, in Pickaway County, Ohio.

Mr. Barr crossed the plains and mountains to Oregon in 1852, which was both difficult and dangerous. He returned seven years afterward (in 1859) to take his family out to Oregon. Since going to Oregon he has at various times filled positions of public trust. He was justice of the peace in Portland in the early sixties. He was also elected as notary public a number of times. In 1873 he received the appointment of collector of customs, and inspector of Shoal Water Bay, which position he held until 1879. He died November 2, 1880, the day James A. Garfield was elected president. He gave good evidence of his acceptance of Christ, and would often speak of a glorious reunion with loved ones in heaven. In politics he was a Republican.

The children born to this union were—

1 THADDEUS STEVENS BARR.[4]
2 ZERELDA JANE BARR.[4]
3 EMMA REBECCA BARR.[4]
4 EFFIE RURAL BARR.[4]
5 WILLIAM LINCOLN BARR.[4]
6 FRANK SHELDON BARR.[4]
7 JESSIE MITCHELL BARR.[4]

1 THADDEUS STEVENS BARR.[4]

1 THADDEUS STEVENS BARR[4] was born July 21, 1850, in Van Buren County, Iowa, and was married to Miss PHOEBE MAJORS, December 4, 1882, at Grays River, Washington, where they live. They have three children.

MURIEL BARR,[5] born in 1884.

OLIVE AMY BARR,[5] born in 1886.

MARGARET MARY BARR,[5] born in 1893.

2 ZERELDA JANE BARR.[4]

2 ZERELDA JANE BARR[4] was born October 19, 1852, in Davis County, Iowa. She was married to Mr. DEWITT HAMILTON JONES August 1, 1871. They have three children.

CLARENCE HOWARD JONES,[5] born July 31 1872. He married EVA EVANGELINE RODGERS at Oregon City, May 18. 1897

BERTHA JONES,[5] born April 4, 1874.

SUZA M. JONES,[5] born March 10, 1881, lives at 448 Clay Street, Portland, Oregon.

3 EMMA REBECCA BARR.[4]

3 EMMA REBECCA BARR[4] was born February 20, 1862, at Portland, Oregon. She is single, and lives with her mother at Grays River, Washington. We are much indebted to Miss Emma for this excellent report of the family, after we had despaired of getting their history.

4 EFFIE RURAL BARR.[4]

4 EFFIE RURAL BARR[4] was born October 14, 1863. She was married to A. T. SEELEY in April, 1878. They have two children.

JAMES D. SEELEY,[5] born in 1882.

HATTIE M SEELEY,[5] born in 1884.

Their present address is Grays River, Washington.

5 WILLIAM LINCOLN BARR.[4]

5 WILLIAM LINCOLN BARR[4] was born August 21, 1865, and was married to JESSIE MAJORS in February, 1891. They have four children.

WILLIAM M. BARR,[5] born in 1893.

SAMUEL DEWITT BARR,[5] born in 1895.

LOUIS BARR,[5] born in 1896.

RUTH BARR,[5] born in 1898.

Their address is Grays River, Washington.

6 FRANK SHELDON BARR.[4]

6 FRANK SHELDON BARR[4] was born June 25, 1870.   His address is Grays River, Washington.

7 JESSIE MITCHELL BARR.[4]

7 JESSIE MITCHELL BARR[4] was born November 6, 1872. She was married to GEORGE S. HOPKINS August 21, 1892. They have three children.

SHERIDAN HOPKINS,[5] born in 1893.

FLORENCE HOPKINS,[5] born in 1896.

FRANK HOPKINS,[5] born in 1898.

Their address is Olympia, Washington.

There are just fifty names in this one family, which is numerically one of the largest.   We wish we knew more of the family as a whole.

IX DAVID BARR.[3]

9 DAVID BARR[3] was born June 14, 1815.   He was married to JANE ALEXANDER BARR, of Center County, Pennsylvania, daughter of William Wills and Jane (Semple) Barr, September 26, 1844, by Rev. William Adams.

After marriage they lived for a few years in Center County, Pennsylvania, near Boalsburg.   They moved from there to Mercer County in 1849, and from there to Lee County, Iowa, in the fall of 1860.   In the fall of 1865 they moved to Fountain Green, Hancock County, Illinois.   Uncle died August 23, 1870, at Humboldt, Kansas, of typhoid fever.   He followed farming most of his life.   Early in life he expressed a desire to study for the ministry, but his father thought he could not furnish the means to educate him, having a family of eleven children for which to provide.   There were born to them eight children.

1 LYDIA E. BARR.[4]
2 NANNIE J. BARR.[4]
3 JOHN X. BARR.[4]
4 ANNA M. BARR.[4]
5 MARY A. BARR.[4]
6 LAURA A. BARR.[4]
7 Infant son, born February 20, 1861, died March 9, 1861.
8 WILLIAM J. BARR.[4]

1 LYDIA E. BARR.[4]

1 LYDIA E BARR[4] was born July 9, 1845, at Boalsburg, Pennsylvania. She was married to JOHN S. DUFFY by Rev. James R. Bell, November 15, 1871. They had two children.

CHARLEY GRAY DUFFY,[5] born in 1872, and died in 1878, aged six years.

IVA MAY DUFFY,[5] born in 1882, and is at home with her mother at Waverly, Kansas.

After Mr. and Mrs. Duffy were married they lived on their farm near Carthage, Illinois, for five years. They then moved to the city of Carthage, where Mr Duffy ran a livery stable until October, 1879, when he sold out and moved to Coffey County, Kansas, where they expect to spend the rest of their days.

Mr. Duffy enlisted in the army in 1862, in Company A, 118th Illinois Mounted Infantry, and served to the close of the war, and was honorably discharged the fall of 1865.

2 NANNIE J. BARR.[4]

2 NANNIE J. BARR[4] was born September 15, 1846, and makes her home with her mother, in Carthage, Illinois. She is a good, kind-hearted lady, and takes care of her mother, who is now eighty years of age, and hence fills an important sphere.

3 JOHN X. BARR.[4]

3 JOHN X. BARR[4] was born April 22, 1848. He enlisted
in the one-hundred-day volunteers, Forty fifth Regiment of Iowa
National Volunteer Infantry, in May, 1864. He died on the
transport on his way home, fifteen miles below Keokuk,
September 16, 1864, and is buried in the cemetery at Keokuk,
Iowa.

4 ANNA M. BARR.[4]

4 ANNA M. BARR[4] was born March 31, 1850. She was
married to Hon. O. F. BERRY, by Rev. Mr. Walker, March
5, 1873.

Mr. Berry was born in McDonough County, Illinois.
Their home at present is in Carthage, Illinois. He has a beautiful home. He is an admirer of good horses, and has some fine
blooded stock. His father was a poor man, and died when
Mr. Berry was a boy. Hence his early life was anything but
rosy. If there is such a thing as self-made men, he is one of
them. He worked on the farm in the summer, and attended
district school during the winter months. Two years after his
father's death his loving mother, who was so shocked by the
death of her husband, died also, and the children were left to
make their own way. That Mr. Berry succeeded in doing so
is very evident.

Having settled on law as his profession after graduating,
and having been admitted to the bar, he moved to Carthage
and opened an office with such success as might be the envy of
any man in the profession. He was the first mayor of the city,
elected after a hard political contest; but the two succeeding
terms he was elected without opposition. During his administration the town passed from a village to a city of the second class.
His own town paper says of him: "It can be truly said that
Mr. Berry has greatly aided in making Carthage what it is

to-day. He is a man with a strong will, clear business fore-thought, and with nerve and capital to back his judgment."

He has for twelve years been State senator from his district; and in 1892, when the Democratic party swept the State, he was returned—although a Republican—by a splendid majority. He is now general attorney for the insurance depart-ment of the State of Illinois, a most important position, and one he ably fills. While a member of the Senate he was the author of the present revenue law of 1899. He was chairman of special Senate committee to investigate Chicago police in 1897, also chairman of committee to examine books of the University of Illinois.

He is a member of the board of trustees of Carthage College, and is the lecturer on civil government and commercial law in that institution. For fifteen years of Mr. Berry's life he has been superintendent of the Sabbath-school of the Presbyter-ian Church, of which he and his wife are members. When he took charge of it, the average attendance was about one hun-dred; and to-day it is five hundred. He has a fine Sunday-school orchestra of thirteen pieces. He is a natural leader, and whether in the home, the church, or political life, he shows himself a true man and gentleman, and wins the confidence of friend and foe.

His wife has been a great help to him and is a woman of superior grace and good sense. They have had with all their honors and advancement many sad days. Their issue, consist-ing of five children, are all dead.

EDITH IRENE BERRY,[5] born December 3, 1873, and died December 30, 1873.

CLARENCE LEE BERRY,[5] born November 11, 1874, and died June 14, 1888.

CHARLES KEITH BERRY,[5] born July 11, 1879, and died August 18, 1879.

WALTER DEAN BERRY,[5] born August 27, 1880, and died
    December 19, 1880.

ORVILLE FRANK BERRY,[5] born October 19, 1882, and died
    August 31, 1896.

They have adopted a little girl, who we trust will fill a
vacancy and be a joy to them.   We are glad to give so much
space to so worthy a family.

5 MARY A. BARR.[4]

5 MARY A. BARR[4] was born January 24, 1852.   She was
married to Mr. WILLIAM J. CAMPBELL April 28, 1870, by the
Rev. Mr. Bell.   They live at present at La Harpe, Illinois.
He is a farmer.   They had one son, C. C. CAMPBELL.   Mr.
W. J. Campbell died July 5, 1894.

6 LAURA A. BARR.[4]

6 LAURA A. BARR[4] was born March 5, 1855, and was
married to Mr. WILLIAM J. DUFFY by Rev. Waldenny, January
19, 1879.   Mr. and Mrs. Duffy live about a mile from Waverly,
Kansas, on their own farm.   After their marriage they lived
in Hancock County, Illinois, till March, 1883, when they
moved to Kansas, and bought Prospect Heights dairy farm.   It
has a living spring of excellent water on it.   Mr. Duffy rents
the farming land and gives his whole attention to the dairy business.   They have one son.

DAVID DEAN DUFFY,[5] born December 4, 1885.

8 WILLIAM J. BARR.[4]

8 WILLIAM J. BARR[4] was born November 10, 1863, and
died at Grand Junction, Colorado, December 1, 1891.

This family are all members of the church, and for the
most part the Presbyterian Church.   They are all well to do,
and enjoy the blessing of God on their substance and their souls.

Mrs. Anna M. Berry.

(Page 144.)

"May the peace of God, that passeth all understanding, keep
their minds and hearts through Christ Jesus."

X ELIZABETH BARR.[3]

10 ELIZABETH BARR,[3] the youngest daughter of grandfather's
family, is still living at Indiana, Pennsylvania. She was born
June 14, 1819. She married Mr. JAMES ANDERSON March 23,
1848. Mr. James Anderson was a son of John and Nancy
(Reed) Anderson. Uncle James was born at Racetown
Branch, Huntingdon County, Pennsylvania, about eight miles
south-west of Huntingdon, June 5, 1824. They were members
of the Associate Church in Huntingdon. (The church was dis-
continued many years ago.) They often walked to church
eight miles over the hills. That would kill the people now,
but the Anderson family were devout Christians and endured
hardness for Christ's sake and his cause.

James Anderson followed the restaurant or confectionery
business all his life, and always made a comfortable living at it.
He was very honest and conscientious in business, and every
person who knew him trusted him; hence he drew about him
the better class of customers. While he was careful never to
neglect his business, he likewise never neglected his church or
family duties. He raised his family strictly and instructed them
carefully. He did not say to his children *you go* to church and
Sabbath-school, but he took them by the hand and said *come*.
He always closed his business on Sabbath day, although others
in the same business found good excuses for keeping open.
When they boasted of what they had made on the Lord's day,
he reproved them for breaking God's law and imperiling their
own souls. He is still doing business, while the others, one
after another, have failed. He is over eighty years old, and is
getting feeble. It is more of such sturdy, determined men of
conviction this age needs, and the church needs. After their

marriage Uncle James and wife removed to Plumville, Pennsylvania, and in 1850 to Indiana, Pennsylvania. After some years he removed from Indiana to LaSalle, Illinois, where he lived a year, and then returned to Indiana. In 1869 he removed to Boonesboro, Iowa, where he remained for fifteen months, and then returned to Indiana, and has since remained there.

Aunt Elizabeth is one of the kindest of women and the best of mothers, always most cheerful and hospitable. She is very feeble now. May their life be as "the path of the just, that shineth more and more unto the perfect day." Uncle James Anderson for years was an elder in the First Presbyterian Church, and when the church divided he went into the Second Church, where he is still an elder.

Their children consist of three daughters and two sons.

1 Nannie Anderson.[4]
2 Samuel Barr Anderson.[4]
3 John T. Anderson.[4]
4 Martha L. Anderson.[4]
5 Jennie H. Anderson.[4]

1 NANNIE ANDERSON.[4]

1 Nannie Anderson[4] was born at Racetown Branch, December 3, 1848. She is single, and keeps house for her parents. She is a good, devoted Christian girl, and is filling a very important mission. She will have her reward.

2 SAMUEL BARR ANDERSON.[4]

2 Samuel Barr Anderson[4] was born October 17, 1850, at Racetown Branch, Huntingdon County, Pennsylvania. He was married to Emma Katherine Bardolph in September, 1873, in Indiana, Pennsylvania. He followed the restaurant business for a while at Blairsville, Pennsylvania. From there

he moved to Middletown, Pennsylvania, then to Johnstown, Pennsylvania, and from there to Pittsburg, Pennsylvania. After going to Pittsburg he was employed in the Oliver Steel Works as bolt inspector. He died in the South Side Hospital of Bright's disease, February 18, 1898. She died in 1892. They were both members of the United Presbyterian Church. To them were born two sons.

> GEORGE BOADENHAMMER ANDERSON[5] was born at Blairs-ville, Pennsylvania. He works in the Oliver Steel Works, Pittsburg. He is married.

> JAMES HERBERT ANDERSON[5] was born at Blairsville, Penn-sylvania. He is a wholesale grocer in Pittsburg, Penn-sylvania. He is married to LETTY ROBINS.

3 JOHN T. ANDERSON.[4]

3 JOHN T. ANDERSON[4] was born October 22, 1852, in Indiana, Pennsylvania. He is with his father, and takes charge of the business. He never married. He is a very genial, good-hearted man, and an active member of the Second United Presbyterian Church.

4 MARTHA L. ANDERSON.[4]

4 MARTHA L. ANDERSON[4] was born July 22, 1855, in LaSalle, Illinois. She was married to JOHN H. STEWART, of DuBois, Pennsylvania, in May, 1884. They have one daughter.

> MABEL E. STEWART,[5] born in DuBois, June 25, 1890.

Mrs. Stewart was a jolly girl, good looking, and good company, and no doubt fills her place well both in the home and in the church.

5 JENNIE H. ANDERSON.[4]

5 JENNIE H. ANDERSON[4] was born July 21, 1858, in Indiana, Pennsylvania. She followed dress-making for a while in Indiana, but decided she would prefer some other kind of

life to that, and was married to Mr. M. M. HAWK, of Apollo, Pennsylvania, by the writer, at New Brighton, Pennsylvania, December 2, 1890. Mr. Hawk was born in 1856. They live about one mile from Paulton, Pennsylvania. Mr. Hawk is employed in the lumber business. He was born in Indiana County, Pennsylvania. To them were born five children.

HAZEL STORY HAWK[5], born October 27, 1891.

CLARENCE ANDERSON HAWK,[5] born July 14, 1893.

HERBERT McMATH HAWK,[5] born January 9, 1895.

ARTHUR STEWART HAWK,[5] born September 9, 1897.

HOWARD BARR HAWK,[5] born August 9, 1899.

XI DANIEL BARR.[3]

11 DANIEL BARR[3] was born April 1, 1822, on the old homestead, near the fort, and lived with his father until his death. He got the homestead at his father's death, except that portion which was allotted to my father, James Barr; and they together were to pay the heirs their portion of the estate. He was married to Mrs. MARTHA EDMISTON April 15, 1847, by Rev. David Stewart. Martha Barr was born September 27, 1823, in Huntingdon County, Pennsylvania. They were faithful members of the United Presbyterian Church, of Stone Valley, Pennsylvania. Uncle died June 17, 1865, in his forty-fourth year, of tuberculosis, brought on by a large man falling on him and dislocating his shoulder and hurting him inwardly. His wife still resides on the old place with her son, Joseph E. Barr.

This home was a very pleasant place to visit. Both uncle and aunt were most kind and hospitable. Aunt's table always groaned with good things, and we never failed to accept an invitation or an opportunity to go to Uncle Daniel's. Many a happy evening has the writer spent in that home. It is blessed to look back upon those early days.

Age is bringing its infirmities. Aunt is at present much crippled with rheumatism and walks with a cane. She was left with a large family after uncle's death, but has managed to keep them together and to make a good home for them, and has lived to see them all either in the church militant or the church triumphant. She is one of the best of women and one of the kindest of mothers.

To them were born seven children.

1 SAMUEL WILLS BARR,[4] born February 12, 1848, and died September 9, 1853, from the effect of sunstroke.

2 JOSEPH EDMISTON BARR.[4]

3 LYDIA ELIZABETH BARR.[4]

4 JOHN CALVIN BARR, M. D.[4]

5 MARY EMMA BARR.[4]

6 ELIZA JANE BARR.[4]

7 SARAH AGNES BARR.[4]

2 JOSEPH EDMISTON BARR.[4]

2 JOSEPH E. BARR[4] was born January 21, 1850. He never married. The responsibility of the farm fell largely upon his young shoulders when his father died (he being but fifteen years of age), but he has succeeded well and deserves great credit. He is taking good care of his mother in her declining days, which is one of the noblest of deeds, and shows him to be a man of good principles.

He is a genial, kind-hearted man to everybody. He takes great interest in the church, as do all the family. He has led the singing in the church much of the time for twenty-five years. He has also been a teacher in the Sabbath-school for many years. He has kept the altar fires of the home burning since his father's death, which is much to say of any young man. He is a Republican in politics, and takes considerable interest in local politics.

3 LYDIA ELIZABETH BARR.[4]

3 LYDIA ELIZABETH BARR[4] was born June 17, 1852. She was married to JOHN E. MAGILL, a son of James W. Magill, who is a brother of the Rev. John A. Magill, so well known to the United Presbyterian Church. His father was an efficient elder in the church for many years. There is a large connection of Magills in that valley, all very respectable people and all connected with that church. Mr. John E. Magill is a brother of Rev. David E. Magill, of Welda, Kansas, who has done a good work. Mr. Magill and family live on the farm owned by his father, two miles north of McAlevy's Fort. They have seven children, all living.

CARRIE J. MAGILL,[5] born March 28, 1878.
SARAH AGNES MAGILL,[5] born January 20, 1880.
SAMUEL CALVIN MAGILL,[5] born September 20, 1881.
WILLIAM BARR MAGILL,[5] born May 1, 1882.
DAVID E. MAGILL,[5] born July 14, 1889.
JOSEPH VERNON MAGILL,[5] born August 22, 1892.
MARY E. MAGILL,[5] born March 19, 1896.

4 JOHN CALVIN BARR, M. D.[4]

4 JOHN C. BARR, M. D.,[4] was born August 14, 1854, and was married to MARY E. WILSON, only daughter of John A. and Nancy (Cummins) Wilson, by Rev. John M. Adair, on September 22, 1876. Mr. Wilson bought my father's farm, and at his death willed it to his daughter and her husband. They own their beautiful home in the fort, where the doctor has his office and practice.

Dr. Barr lived on the farm with his brother Joseph until after he was married. He then attended lectures for three years at Baltimore, graduating from the University of Maryland April 8, 1889, having completed a full course, and receiving an honorable diploma. He also received from this institution two certificates on specialties ; one on throat and chest diseases, and one on obstetrics.   The same fall he entered the Jefferson Medical College of Philadelphia, from which he graduated April 8, 1890, receiving an honorable diploma.   He has been practicing with good success in his home village, McAlevy's Fort, Pennsylvania, ever since.

Their children are as follows :

JOHN WALTER BARR,[5] born November 23, 1878.   He is a promising young man, and has been teaching school for some years very successfully.

AZILA CUMMINS BARR,[5] born April 5, 1880.   She is also quite bright, and teaches school during the winter season. She is at home with her mother when not teaching.   She is also quite proficient in music.

They have three infants dead, respectively, MAY, JUNE, and ROY.

LAURA AGNES BARR,[5] born April 7, 1892, is a bright, wide-awake girl.

5 MARY EMMA BARR.[4]

5 MARY EMMA BARR,[4] was born August 26, 1857, and died July 15, 1874.   She got a fall when a child, which injured her spine, and she was a great care as long as she lived.

6 ELIZA JANE BARR.[4]

6 ELIZA JANE BARR[4] was born August 25, 1860.   She died May 19, 1894, of typhoid pneumonia.   She was an earnest member of the church.

7 SARAH AGNES BARR.[4]

7 SARAH AGNES BARR,[4] the youngest child, was born October 18, 1864, and lived at home until she was married to WILLIAM CUMMINS, son of John Cummins, January 23, 1896. They own a store in McAlevy's Fort.   They are both members of the United Presbyterian Church.   They have no children.

This concludes the record of SAMUEL BARR,[2] the fourth family. We have given a somewhat lengthy report of this family, on account of being familiar with the members of it. It would not be modest in the writer to praise this large family, of which he is a member. Suffice it to say, he is not ashamed of his company. The record speaks for itself. There are 320 members of the family. Eleven took part in the Civil War; seven entered the ministry; four, the practice of medicine.

John Calvin Barr, M. D.

(Page 152.)

FAMILY V.

GABRIEL BARR.[2]

GABRIEL BARR[2] was the fifth and youngest son of ROBERT BARR.[1] He came to this country with his father in 1790, and settled in East Kishacoquillas Valley, Mifflin County, Pennsylvania.

He married Miss MARY WILLS, of Mifflin County, a daughter of John Wills. It is a strange coincident that he married a lady of the same name and connection as his father, although he married in America, and his father in Ireland. Mr. Barr died in Mifflin County. We have no record of his birth or death.

His wife had three brothers, John, Samuel and Hugh; and two sisters, Mary and Elizabeth. After her husband's death, Mrs. Barr with her family, and her father and mother, brothers and sisters, moved to Chillicothe, Ohio, in 1802.

To them were born four children.

    I JOHN WILLS BARR.[3]
    II MARGARET BARR.[3]
    III WILLIAM BARR.[3]
    IV GABRIEL BARR.[3]

I JOHN WILLS BARR.[3]

1 JOHN WILLS BARR[3] was born about 1792. He married Miss MARTHA HEMPHILL. They moved to Richland County, near Lexington, Ohio. He died near Mansfield, Ohio, in 1828, when he was about thirty-six years of age. He was a farmer. He left a wife and four children. She married again.

The children are as follows:

    1 JANE BARR.[4]
    2 ELIZABETH BARR.[4]
    3 MARY ANN BARR.[4]
    4 HENRY BARR.[4]

1 JANE BARR.[4]

1 JANE BARR,[4] the eldest daughter, married a man by the name of HENRY WINTERSTEIN. She is dead. Little is known of the family. They had one daughter and one son.

    1 HARRIET ADELINE WINTERSTEIN.[5]
    2 CLINTON BARR WINTERSTEIN.[5]

1 HARRIET A. WINTERSTEIN.[5]

1 HARRIET A. WINTERSTEIN[5] was born in Richland County, Ohio, March 22, 1841. She was married to JOHN B. RITCHIE February 13, 1862. His occupation is farming. They live at Bloomfield, Iowa. They have four children.

    JENNIE M. RITCHIE[6] was born in Richland County, Ohio, November 26, 1862. She married Mr. HOTCHKISS.

    ANNIE E. RITCHIE[6] was born in Richland County, Ohio, March 26, 1864. She married Mr. HESKETT.

    ALLIE B. RITCHIE[6] was born in Davis County, Iowa, August 3, 1866.

    WILLIAM H. RITCHIE[6] was born in Davis County, Iowa, September 5, 1869.

2 CLINTON BARR WINTERSTEIN.[5]

2 CLINTON B. WINTERSTEIN[5] was born in Richland County, Ohio. He lives at Wahpeton, North Dakota. He was a small child when his mother died.

He enlisted in the Civil War, and when he came home he found he had lost all claim to his mother's estate. He says he is proud of his mother's name, for it was the only thing of her's he ever inherited. He never married.

2 ELIZABETH BARR.[4]

2 ELIZABETH BARR[4] was born in 1828, four months after her father's death. She married SAMUEL FLEMING, of Richland

ADDENDA.

[This matter came too late to be inserted in its proper place.]

W. B. FLEMING.[5]

W. B. FLEMING[5] was born April 4, 1849. He enlisted in the Civil war in Company A, 187th Ohio Volunteers, under Captain W. W. Cockley.

His father, Samuel K. Fleming, was born September 13, 1818, in Pennsylvania. He married ELIZABETH BARR[4] July 8, 1848. He died July 31, 1891, and she died July 28, 1850.

Mr. Samuel K. Fleming was married the second time to ELLEN STEEBY, December 27, 1860. Mr. Fleming and his first wife were members of the old-school Presbyterian Church. He was a deacon until his second marriage. After his second marriage he and his wife united with the Congregational Church.

Mr. W. B. Fleming married Miss CAROLINE THUME in Lexington, Ohio, November 17, 1870. She was born May 7, 1849. Mr. Fleming has followed railroading for twenty-five years. He has been on the A. T. & S. F. Railroad for fourteen years, making his home at Newton, Kansas. He owns a farm in Konantz, Colorado, where he now lives, having given up railroading in 1900. He is in the cattle business and doing well.

To them were born seven children, all living but one.

1 ROLLIN D. FLEMING[6] was born June 4, 1872. He married Miss BIRDIE GILLESPIE June 13, 1885. They have four children, three sons and one daughter.

2 CLINTON F. FLEMING[6] was born August 4, 1874.

3 JUDD A. FLEMING[6] was born November 22, 1876.

4 ELLA M. FLEMING[6] was born June 18, 1879.

5 MARY GRACE FLEMING[6] was born October 4, 1885. She died August 23, 1887.

6 CHARLES T. FLEMING[6] was born October 4, 1887.

7 EARL JAY FLEMING[6] was born June 29, 1892.

County, Ohio. She died about 1850. To them were born two children.

An infant that died in infancy.

WILLIAM F. FLEMING,[5] lives at Newton, Kansas. He is a saddler by trade.

3 MARY ANN BARR.[4]

3 MARY ANN BARR[4] was born April 12, 1824, and died February 23, 1877. She and her brother Henry went to live with her Grandfather Hemphill after their father's death. When their grandfather died they went to live with their Uncle John and Aunt Sarah Johnston, where Mary lived until she married. She was married to EDWARD JOHNSTON October 14, 1847. He was born August 6, 1823, and died March 19, 1886. They left two sons and one daughter.

1 HENRY CLINTON JOHNSTON.[5]
2 JOSEPH J. JOHNSTON.[5]
3 SARAH CATHARINE JOHNSTON.[5]

1 HENRY CLINTON JOHNSTON.[5]

1 HENRY CLINTON JOHNSTON[5] was born December 13, 1853. He was married to NANCY POLING December 2, 1875. He is a farmer at Bremen, Ohio. They have five children.

CHLOE MAUD JOHNSTON,[6] born February 26, 1879.
JOSEPH FRANKLIN JOHNSTON,[6] born May 6, 1881.
EDWARD RAY JOHNSTON,[6] born March 5, 1883.
WILLIAM CLOID JOHNSTON,[6] born September 7, 1885.
HARRY BRUSH JOHNSTON,[6] born August 26, 1887.

2 JOSEPH J. JOHNSTON.[5]

2 JOSEPH J. JOHNSTON[5] was born August 24, 1858. He was married to MARGARET POLING September 30, 1884. He is a farmer at Bremen, Ohio. They have no children.

3 SARAH CATHARINE JOHNSTON.[5]

3 SARAH CATHARINE JOHNSTON[5] was born February 24, 1851. She married CHARLES FRANKLIN SPEICE October 13, 1870. He was born January 26, 1850. They were both born and married in Fairfield County, Ohio. They lived in McComb County, Ohio, for eighteen years, and moved last April (1900) to their present home, in Findlay, Ohio. Mr. Speice is engaged in the manufacturing business, and has oil interests. Their children are as follows:

EDWARD JOHNSTON SPEICE[6] was born September 27, 1873. He is a graduate in pharmacy from Ada (Ohio) University and lives in Fostoria, Ohio. He served for one year as hospital steward in the Sixth Ohio Volunteer Infantry during the Spanish-American War. Part of the time he was in Cuba. He is single.

JENNIE SPEICE[6] was born June 27, 1873. She married Mr. JOSEPH WASSON, a banker in McComb, Ohio, August 23, 1892. They have two children.

RHEA WASSON,[7] born May 24, 1895.

ROLAND WASSON,[7] born February 19, 1896.

WILLIAM CLINTON SPEICE[6] was born March 6, 1875. He married LAURA SEYMORE, of Elwood, Indiana. He is a graduate of Peoria, Illinois, in optics and watch-making.

STELLA SPEICE[6] was born November 17, 1878, and died January 22, 1892. She lost her life at Indianapolis, Indiana, during that terrible fire at the National Surgical Institute, while there undergoing treatment for hip disease. She was a most beautiful and lovely girl, and had a host of friends to mourn her death.

CHARLES FLOYD SPEICE[6] was born October 18, 1883. He is in college at Findlay, taking a classical course.

RUTH SPEICE[6] was born November 16, 1892.

4 HENRY BARR.[4]

4 HENRY BARR,[4] son of JOHN WILLS BARR,[3] was born in Richland County, Ohio, June 16, 1826. He lived in Richland County with his Grandfather Hemphill until he was nine years of age. After his grandfather's death, he went to live with his Uncle Johnston, in Richland County, Ohio, and there remained until he was eighteen years of age.

He then went to Somerset, Perry County, Ohio, to learn the trade of blacksmithing. This he followed for eleven years. During this time he married EMMA ASHBAUGH, of Fairfield County, in the year 1852. She was born November 24, 1826, in the aforesaid county. Here they lived until the year 1864, when they removed to Hancock County, Indiana.

Here Mr. Barr enlisted in the Civil War, February 10, 1865, serving about six months, or until the close of the war, August 4, 1865. He was in Company H, 147th Regiment Indiana Volunteers. After his return from the army he removed to Blackford County, Indiana. He followed farming after 1855, until his death, at Millgrove, Blackford County, Indiana, to which place he had removed in 1891, to spend his remaining days in retirement. He died October 31, 1892. His wife still survives him. In politics he was first a Whig, and later a Republican.

To this union were born five children.

1 MARTHA E. BARR.[5]
2 DURINDA J. BARR.[5]
3 FLORENCE G. BARR.[5]
4 AUGUSTA M. BARR.[5]
5 CHARLES W. BARR.[5]

1 MARTHA E. BARR.[5]

1 MARTHA E. BARR[5] was born February 23, 1853, in Fairfield County, Ohio. She was married to Dr. JOHN W. SAGE,

of Blackford County, Indiana, in July, 1869. Her husband followed his practice in Hartford City, Blackford County, Indiana, until his death, December 10, 1899. He served three years in the Civil War, and was honorably discharged. To them were born seven children.

HARRY A. SAGE,[6] born March 27, 1871.

ERNEST D. SAGE,[6] born May 10, 1875, killed June 10, 1898, by lightning.

FREDERICK A. SAGE,[6] born November 17, 1879.

NELLIE G. SAGE,[6] born March 1, 1882.

HOWARD H. SAGE,[6] born October 16, 1884.

RUTH F. SAGE,[6] born in August, 1888.

EDITH P. SAGE,[6] born January 28, 1891.

2 DURINDA J. BARR.[5]

2 DURINDA J. BARR[5] was born March 29, 1856. She married DAVID VANCE, of Blackford County, Indiana, July 22, 1878. He was a carpenter by trade until the year 1878, when he moved on a farm, and has since followed that business. He also served four years in the Civil War. No children were born to this union.

3 FLORENCE G. BARR.[5]

3 FLORENCE G. BARR[5] was born June 16, 1862, and was married to Mr. MARION BARTLETT, of Delaware County, Indiana, in February, 1883. Her husband followed farming and tile making in the States of Indiana and Illinois until 1889, since which time they have resided in Blackford County, Indiana, and are extensively engaged in gardening and fruit growing. To them were born seven children.

CLIFFORD BARTLETT.[6]

HOMER BARTLETT.[6]

ALMA L. BARTLETT.[6]

NORA BARTLETT.[6]

NELLIE BARTLETT.[6]
WILLARD BARTLETT.[6]
Infant son.
All are living except the infant son.

4 AUGUSTA M. BARR.[5]

4 AUGUSTA M. BARR[5] was born March 22, 1864. She was married to EDWIN M. SHROYER, of Blackford County, Indiana, in October, 1886. Her husband follows farming and raising of thorough-bred sheep. To this union were born five children.

RUSSEL SHROYER,[6] born September 6, 1888.
Infant Son.
GUY SHROYER.[6]
OPAL SHROYER,[6] born November 2, 1893.
CHESTER SHROYER.[6]
All are dead except Russel and Opal.

5 CHARLES W. BARR.[5]

5 CHARLES W. BARR[5] was born July 23, 1867, and was married to HANNAH L. SHRACK, of Blackford County, Indiana, October 17, 1891. He was raised on the farm and still follows that business during the summer season, and teaches during the winter season, having taught for twelve consecutive terms. To this union were born three children.

R. FERNLEY BARR,[6] born January 25, 1894.
GOLDIE J. BARR,[6] born January 13, 1896.
MARCIA A. BARR,[6] born March 7, 1899.
All are living.

This closes the record of JOHN WILLS BARR'S[8] family and descendants. We are sorry it is not more complete. If anything comes in later it will appear in the Supplement.

II MARGARET BARR.[3]

2 MARGARET BARR[3] was born probably about 1798, in Mifflin County, Pennsylvania. She was the only daughter of GABRIEL BARR.[2] She went with the family to Chillicothe, Ohio, in 1802. She married WILLIAM McWILLIAMS. They lived in Richland County, Ohio, near Lexington. Mr. McWilliams died fifty years ago.

To them were born two sons and one daughter.

GABRIEL McWILLIAMS.[4]

WILLIAM McWILLIAMS.[4]

MARY ANN McWILLIAMS.[4] She married Mr. HARRISON PAYNE.

After much correspondence this was all we were able to learn about this family. If anything comes later it will be found in the Supplement.

III WILLIAM BARR.[3]

3 WILLIAM BARR,[3] the second son of GABRIEL BARR,[2] was born March 5, 1800, in Mifflin County, Pennsylvania. He was married to MARY BROWN, daughter of David Brown, March 24, 1829. She was born December 17, 1807.

Mr. Barr came with his mother and family to Chillicothe, Ohio, in 1802. He died April 29, 1849. His wife died August 5, 1853, in Fairfield County, Ohio. He was a very ingenious man, a farmer and a wheelwright. Their family consisted of three sons and two daughters.

1 MARY ELIZABETH BARR.[4]

2 DAVID ALEXANDER BARR.[4]

3 JOHN WILLS BARR.[4]

4 MARGARET JANE BARR.[4]

5 WILLIAM CALVIN BARR.[4]

Mr. David A. Barr.

(Page 164.)

1 MARY ELIZABETH BARR.[4]

1 MARY ELIZABETH BARR[4] was born near West Rushville, Fairfield County, Ohio, November 9, 1831. She was married August 26, 1852, to JOHN P. BOGLE, of Perry County, Ohio. Mr. Bogle was born in 1824.

They now live in Augusta, Butler County, Kansas. They are members of the Methodist Episcopal Church, because there is no United Presbyterian Church in reach of them. They have had four sons and three daughters.

1 WILLIAM CALVIN BOGLE[5] was born January 15, 1854, in Perry County, Ohio. He is single.

2 MARGARET AMELIA BOGLE.[5]

3 SARAH ADA BOGLE.[5]

4 JAMES BOGLE[5] was born October 31, 1863, and died October 16, 1864.

5 JOHN YOST BOGLE.[5]

6 SAMUEL STEWART BOGLE.[5]

7 FRANKIE BOGLE,[5] born October 6, 1871, in Butler County, Kansas, and died July 17, 1874.

2 MARGARET AMELIA BOGLE.[5]

2 MARGARET AMELIA BOGLE[5] was born August 3, 1857, in Perry County, Ohio. She was married to H. LOVELL BLUE December 5, 1877. To them were born seven children.

ADA BLUE,[6] born November 8, 1878, died January 11, 1880.

CALVIN BLUE,[6] born January 16, 1882.

HARRY BLUE,[6] born August 30, 1884.

JAMES BLUE,[6] born August 30, 1886.

ARTEMUS BLUE,[6] born May 26, 1889.

REBECCA E. BLUE, born March 26, 1892.

JOHN F. BLUE,[6] born May 26, 1896.

3 SARAH ADA BOGLE.[5]

3 SARAH ADA BOGLE[5] was born December 10, 1860. She married LEONARD M. HONCE December 25, 1890. He died in June, 1893. To them were born two children.

CLARENCE HONCE,[6] born March 7, 1892, died June 20, 1892.

WALTER HONCE,[6] born May 11, 1893, died October 17, 1893.

5 JOHN YOST BOGLE.[5]

5 JOHN YOST BOGLE[5] was born July 26, 1865. He married CHESSIE SPARKS December 28, 1888. To them were born two children.

GRACIE BOGLE,[6] born January 12, 1897.

MABEL BOGEL,[6] born November 5, 1889.

6 SAMUEL STEWART BOGLE.[5]

6 SAMUEL STEWART BOGLE[5] was born December 27, 1868, in Perry County, Ohio. He married EFFIE CAUSEA November 1, 1893. They have one child.

ROSA BOGLE,[6] born December 5, 1894.

2 DAVID ALEXANDER BARR.[4]

2 DAVID ALEXANDER BARR[4] was born September 14, 1833, and lives on the farm where he was born, in sight of the Tent Church, near West Rushville, Fairfield County, Ohio. He married MATILDA MARTIN, who was born December 8, 1836. She was the daughter of John M. Martin, who was born May 14, 1796, and died September 9, 1858. He was a soldier in the War of 1812.

They were married April 24, 1856. She died November 7, 1880. Mr. Barr has been an elder in the West Rushville United Presbyterian Church since June 13, 1873. We are under great obligations to this cousin for the great pains and trouble to which he went to gather the history of this branch of the family

To them were born eight children.

1 JAMES AUSTIN BARR.[5]
2 ALMA JANE BARR.[5]
3 ESTELLA ISABELLE BARR.[5]
4 ERWIN VINCENT BARR.[5]
5 SARAH MATILDA BARR.[5]
6 ETTA REBECCA BARR.[5]
7 ARTHUR CLARENCE BARR.[5]
8 Infant, died in infancy, eight days before the mother.

1 JAMES AUSTIN BARR.[5]

1 JAMES AUSTIN BARR[5] was born April 14, 1857. He married ANNA HOUSTON, of Perry County, Ohio, October 10, 1883. They live near Mt. Perry, Perry County, Ohio. To them were born four children.

JOSIE BARR,[6] born November 26, 1884.

MABEL M. BARR,[6] born October 27, 1886, died September 29, 1887.

GOLDIE E. BARR,[6] born January 4, 1889.

LOREA V. BARR,[6] born January 16, 1892.

2 ALMA JANE BARR.[5]

2 ALMA JANE BARR[5] was born May 21, 1860. She has been an invalid for eighteen years, and cannot assist in the home duties. Her part is to suffer.

3 ESTELLA ISABELLE BARR.[5]

3 ESTELLA ISABELLE BARR[5] was born October 21, 1862. She married JOHN G. GINGHER March 27, 1887. They moved to Newbraska, staid one year and a half, came back and settled in Columbus, Ohio, and were members of the First

United Presbyterian Church, Rev. R. B. Patton, pastor. She died November 12, 1896, leaving one little son, born October 20, 1896. She is reported to have been a lovely Christian character.

4 ERWIN VINCENT BARR.[5]

4 ERWIN VINCENT BARR,[5] second son of DAVID A. BARR,[4] was born August 21, 1865. He married MAGGIE BELL POOL February 25, 1891. They have no family. They live at Stautsville, Ohio. He is in the mill and grain business.

5 SARAH MATILDA BARR.[5]

5 SARAH MATILDA BARR[5] was married to U. GRANT BROYLES April 26, 1893. She was born October 6, 1868. They live in Columbus, Ohio. They have no family.

6 ETTA REBECCA BARR.[5]

6 ETTA REBECCA BARR[5] was born September 5, 1870. She is at home and keeps house for her father, and is his standby. So she fills an important place.

7 ARTHUR CLARENCE BARR.[5]

7 ARTHUR CLARENCE BARR[5] was born November 20, 1875. He married MAGGIE D. DAUBENMIRE December 31, 1896. They have one daughter, born August 14, 1898. They live at Stautsville with his brother Vincent. They belong to and attend the home church at West Rushville, Ohio, a distance of twenty-five miles.

3 JOHN WILLS BARR.[4]

3 JOHN WILLS BARR[4] was born January 29, 1836, in Fairfield County, Ohio. He married LUCY McGINNIS December 27, 1860. She was born November 11, 1839. She died December 18, 1878, aged thirty-nine years. He died May 27, 1866. They left one son and one daughter.

Prof. A. M. Bogle.

(Page 168.)

1 Joseph Edson Barr.[5]
2 Sarah Margaret Barr.[5]

I JOSEPH EDSON BARR.[5]

1 Joseph Edson Barr[5] was born March 23, 1863. He married Clara J. Rowel April 10, 1884. He lives on the farm where his father died. They have one son and one daughter living.

Alta R. Barr,[6] born September 2, 1885.

Maggie F. Barr,[6] born March 7, 1888, died December 23, 1888.

William F. Barr,[6] born November 17, 1896.

4 MARGARET JANE BARR.[4]

4 Margaret Jane Barr[4] was born April 14, 1840, in Fairfield County, Ohio. She married Zenos Mitchel Bogle, of Perry County, Ohio, October 14, 1858. He was born March 11, 1833.

They live in Beulah, Crawford County, Kansas, at present. For ten years they lived on the old homestead in Hopewell township, Perry County, Ohio, owned jointly by Zenos Mitchel and an older brother, Erastus. Her husband having sold his interest in the farm to his brother, he bought a farm near Mt. Perry, in the same county, to which they moved in 1869. They were members of Jonathan's Creek United Presbyterian Church, in the bounds of which they lived. In the spring of 1882 they sold the Ohio farm and removed to Crawford County Kansas, where a brother, James Bogle, had preceded them a year, and another brother, Erastus Bogle, followed a year later. They bought and located on a farm on the edge of Sheridan township, about five miles west of Pittsburg, Kansas, where they have resided ever since, with the exception of a short residence in Pittsburg. Mr. Bogle is a ruling elder of the church at Pittsburg, Kansas. There were born to them six children.

    1 ARTEMUS MELVIN BOGLE.[5]
    2 EMMA SARAH BOGLE.[5]
    3 ELMER PRESTON BOGLE.[5]
    4 ESSIE LORENA BOGLE.[5]
    5 HOMES PEARL BOGLE.[5]
    6 FRANK WHITE BOGLE.[5]

1 ARTEMUS MELVIN BOGLE.[5]

1 ARTEMUS MELVIN BOGLE was born in Hopewell township, Perry County, Ohio, March 9, 1860. At the age of fourteen he entered Madison Academy, Mt. Perry, Ohio. After completing the course there, he entered Muskingum College, New Concord, Ohio, graduating classically with the class of 1880, at the age of twenty. In 1889 he graduated from the Latin course of the Kansas State Normal School. In the year 1892-93 he was a special student in mathematics at Cornell University, Ithaca, New York.

He is a teacher by profession, and began his work in the rural schools of Ohio and Kansas, going to the latter place in 1881. Later he was principal of the business department of Tarkio College, Tarkio, Missouri, for three years, 1889-1892. From 1893 to 1897 he was instructor in mathematics and physics in the Susquehanna Collegiate Institute, Towanda, Pennsylvania. Since April, 1899, he has been instructor in mathematics, in the High School, Kansas City, Kansas. He has done some normal institute work also in Kansas.

2 EMMA SARAH BOGLE.[5]

2 EMMA SARAH BOGLE[5] was born March 6, 1862, on the old Barr homestead, Hopewell township, Perry County, Ohio.

She was married to HUGH FINLEY HUSTON, who was born in Muskingum County, Ohio, September 7, 1855. They moved from Ohio in the fall of 1881, locating on a farm four and one-half miles west of Pittsburg, Kansas, where they have lived ever since, and where the last eight children were born. To them were born nine children.

WILLMETTA ESTHER HUSTON[6] was born near Mt. Perry, Ohio, September 19, 1880.

LEONA ETHEL HUSTON[6] was born August 10, 1882, in Baker township, Crawford County, Kansas.

CHAUNCY EVERETT HUSTON,[6] born April 22, 1884.

ANNA ARETHA HUSTON,[6] born March 31, 1886.

DAISY MISSOURI HUSTON,[6] born January 29, 1888.

MARGUERITE REBECCA HUSTON,[6] born March 11, 1890.

VERA LORENA HUSTON,[6] born December 24, 1891.

OLGA VESTA HUSTON,[6] born September 22, 1894.

ROBERT LESTER HUSTON,[6] born December 30, 1896.

3 ELMER PRESTON BOGLE.[5]

3 ELMER PRESTON BOGLE[5] was born in Hopewell township, Crawford County, Kansas, February 28, 1864. He was married to ELIZABETH ELLEN BROWN, of Beulah, Crawford County, Kansas, August 6, 1885. She was born March 6, 1867, at Lebanon, Illinois. He has resided in and near Beulah most of the time since his marriage. His wife died December 5, 1897. She was buried in the cemetery at Beulah. She left two children.

BLANCH FLORENCE BOGLE,[6] born August 29, 1887.

ROY HENDERSON BOGLE,[6] born March 27, 1892.

4 ESSIE LORENA BOGLE.[5]

4 ESSIE LORENA BOGLE[5] was born December 28, 1865, in Hopewell township, Perry County, Ohio. She married

James W. Alexander, of Crawford County, Kansas. He was born May 17, 1860, near Coulterville, Illinois. To them were born four children.

> Floy O. Alexander[6] was born at Coulterville, Illinois, December 15, 1887. Later her parents moved to Pittsburg, Kansas. Here Floy died February 3, 1892.
>
> Veta M. Alexander[6] was born May 29, 1891, at Pittsburg, Kansas.
>
> Donald Bogle Alexander[6] was born March 6, 1895.
>
> Gladys Nellie Alexander[6] was born March 2, 1897, at Vernon, Missouri.

5 HOLMES PEARL BOGLE.[5]

5 Holmes Pearl Bogle[5] was born October 13, 1872, near Mt. Perry, Ohio. She died November 19, 1882, in Crawford County, Kansas.

6 FRANK WHITE BOGLE.[5]

6 Frank White Bogle[5] was born September 6, 1874, near Mt. Perry, Ohio. He was married November 7, 1900, to Ina Asenath Smith, daughter of George A. and Alice Smith, of Beulah, Kansas.

5 WILLIAM CALVIN BARR.[4]

5 William Calvin Barr,[4] youngest son of William Barr,[3] was born June 29, 1843, in Fairfield County, Ohio. He was married to Sarah Ann Hazlett, of Perry County, Ohio, June 29, 1865, by Rev. Moses Floyd. They moved to Lode, Illinois, and stayed there one year. Mrs. Barr died there November 19, 1866, leaving an infant son, now the Rev. R. H. Barr, of Garrattsville, New York.

Rev. Rechnold H. Barr.

(Page 171.)

REV. RECHNOLD HAZLETT BARR.[5]

REV. RECHNOLD HAZLETT BARR[5] was born November 17, 1866. He married MARY BARR, of Conotton, Ohio, May 1, 1895.

Her father's name was Joseph H. Barr; her grandfather, Matthew; and her great-grandfather, Thomas, who came to this country from Ireland late in the eighteenth century. Her great-grandfather married Jennie Patton and to them were born triplets (her grandfather Matthew and his brothers Hugh and Robert), all of whom lived and were taken by aunts (sisters of their father), after the death of their mother, who died in child bed. Later, her grandfather was raised by James Lyons, and the other two by their father and his second wife, who was Sarah McClintock. All three lived to raise large families. Her great-grandfather had no brothers. His sisters married Thomas Stevenson, Robert Stevenson, James Lyons and Samuel Creswell.

I have given this lineage, because it has been thought by some of the friends that this Thomas Barr was one of the connection. I have not been able to connect him. If any of the friends can do so I would be glad to be informed on the matter. (Mrs. Barr's Uncle Thomas W. Barr, of New Rumley, Ohio, furnishes this statement.)

Rev. R. H. Barr was raised by his Grandfather and Grandmother Hazlett, near Mt. Perry, Ohio. His grandmother died in November, 1871, and in 1875 his grandfather married Jane M. Coulter, and with them he lived until he was married.

He was received into the Goshen United Presbyterian Church by Rev. James White, D. D., when thirteen years old. He entered Muskingum College, New Concord, Ohio, September 6, 1887, and graduated from that institution June 23, 1892. He entered Xenia Theological Seminary September 7, 1892, and graduated from that institution April 26, 1895. He was licensed to preach by Xenia Presbytery, May 2, 1894, and was stated supply at Salt Creek until September 1, 1895; also was stated supply of the united charge of East Union and Salt Creek from May, 1895, to September, 1895. He was called to Elvira, Iowa, Le Clair Presbytery, November 17, 1895, and ordained by the Presbytery January 14, 1896. He was very successful there. He was relieved from that field February 22, 1898. He accepted a call to Garrattsville (Delaware Presbytery), New York, in November, 1898, where he is at present.

Two children were born to them.

GEORGE WILBERT BARR,[6] born at Elvira, Ohio, March 13, 1896.

BESSIE CHRISTINE BARR,[6] born at Garrattsville, New York, July 6, 1900.

Mr. William Calvin Barr,[4] after the death of his wife, came back from Illinois to Ohio, and there married MARTHA J. CAHILL, of northern Indiana, October 24, 1867. They had one son and one daughter.

1 GEORGE A. BARR.[5]

2 NORA E. BARR.[5]

1 GEORGE A. BARR.[5]

1 GEORGE A. BARR[5] was born August 9, 1868. He married MINNIE ADAMS November 6, 1889, and lives on a farm at Fountain Head, Tennessee. They have one daughter.

IMOGENE BARR,[6] born at Fountain Head, Tennessee, September 18, 1898.

2 NORA E. BARR.[5]

2 NORA E. BARR[5] was born November 1, 1869, and died May 16, 1872.

Mr. William Calvin Barr after his second marriage moved to the State of Michigan, where he died October 28, 1871.

He enlisted in the Union Army in August, 1861, in Company B, Seventeenth Ohio Volunteer Infantry. He was with Grant's army at the battle of Pittsburg Landing, Tennessee, April 6, 1862. He with six others of his company were detailed to haul ammunition from the river up to the batteries. A most marvelous thing occurred while he was making the second trip. A shell exploded under his team of six mules, killing every one of them, but he did not receive a scratch.

He was kept at teaming until he was discharged, September, 1864. He was never wounded, but he contracted the measles and took cold, and never fully recovered from the effects. His wife was married to Mr. Deeter and lately moved from Fountain Head, Tennessee.

IV GABRIEL BARR.[3]

4 GABRIEL BARR,[3] youngest son of GABRIEL BARR[2] was born in Mifflin County, Pennsylvania, April 20, 1802, and after his father's death moved with the rest of the family to Chillicothe, Ohio, when an infant. He was a farmer. He married Miss MARTHA BROWN in 1826. He died October 17, 1850, at the age of forty-eight. She died January 26, 1875. To them were born eight children, three sons and five daughters.

1 MARY BARR.[4]
2 SAMUEL WILLS BARR.[4]
3 MARGARET BARR.[4]
4 DAVID BROWN BARR.[4]
5 NANCY BARR.[4]
6 ELIZABETH BARR.[4]
7 REBECCA ANN BARR.[4]
8 ROBERT McTEER BARR.[4]

1 MARY BARR.[4]

1 MARY BARR[4] was born February 26, 1827. She was married to Mr. JOHN NEELEY January 10, 1850. He was born

April 15, 1821. They live in Perry County, Ohio. They have four children.

    1 SARAH ELIZABETH NEELEY.[5]
    2 ANNA MARGARET NEELEY.[5]
    3 MARTHA JANE NEELEY.[5]
    4 SILAS BARR NEELEY.[5]

1 SARAH ELIZABETH NEELEY.[5]

1 SARAH E. NEELEY[5] was born October 25, 1856. She married PETER WAGNER October 14, 1875. There were born to them five children.

IRVIN WAGNER,[6] born in 1877.
JOHN O. WAGNER,[6] born in 1879.
CLIFFORD WAGNER,[6] born in 1881.
GRACE WAGNER,[6] born in 1883.
MELVIN WAGNER,[6] born in 1885.

2 ANNA MARGARET NEELEY.[5]

2 ANNA MARGARET NEELEY[5] was born September 28, 1858. She married WATSON GRIGGS August 12, 1879. Three children were born to them.

ORPHY GRIGGS,[6] born in October, 1880.
EARL GRIGGS,[6] born in August, 1882.
DOLPHUS GRIGGS,[6] born in January, 1889.

3 MARTHA JANE NEELEY.[5]

3 MARTHA JANE NEELEY[5] was born December 4, 1851. She married JOHN HENDERSON January 7, 1887. They have one daughter.

LEAH HENDERSON[6] was born in January, 1889.

4 SILAS BARR NEELEY.[5]

4 SILAS BARR NEELEY[5] was born March 19, 1854. He is single and lives with his mother and helps to make a home for her.

This entire family reside in Fairfield and Perry Counties, Ohio.

2 SAMUEL WILLS BARR.[4]

2 SAMUEL WILLS BARR[4] married REBECCA JANE BROWN, in Fairfield County, Ohio, in 1853. She died less than two years after, leaving no children.

He enlisted in the army during the Civil War, and served under General Butler. He died of camp fever in the hospital at New Orleans, in September, 1863.

3 MARGARET BARR.[4]

3 MARGARET BARR[4] was married to WILLIAM MAJOR, at Kirklin, Clinton County, Indiana, in December, 1857. She was a successful school teacher for many years. To them were born seven children.

MARTHA MAJOR[5] died when eighteen years of age.

MARY EMMA MAJOR[5] married WILLIAM GALLAGHER, who with three children survive her and live at Kirklin, Indiana. She died in January, 1900.

FRANCIS MILROY MAJOR[5] died at the age of twenty months.

SAMUEL CHESTER MAJOR[5] married and lives in Indiana. He has no children.

JOHN GLENN MAJOR[5] is unmarried.

ANNA MAY MAJOR[5] died when twenty-one years of age.

ELLA MAUD MAJOR[5] died when three months old.

4 DAVID BROWN BARR.[4]

4 DAVID BROWN BARR,[4] second son of GABRIEL BARR,[3] was born October 24, 1833. He married LOUISA JANE KENNEDY, in Fairfield County, Ohio, January 7, 1858. They live in West Rushville, Ohio. Mr. Eyman has been a ruling elder in the United Presbyterian Church of that place since October 31, 1884. There were born to them two daughters.

MARY ELIZABETH BARR,[5] born October 5, 1864. She is single.

MARTHA LORETTA BARR,[5] born October 7, 1868. She married EDWARD W. EYMAN September 9, 1891. They have three children.

> ELZA CARL EYMAN,[6] born November 3, 1892.
>
> RETNA MERLE EYMAN,[6] born December 31, 1896.
>
> MYRTLE LORIE EYMAN,[6] born April 14, 1900.

5 NANCY BARR.[4]

5 NANCY BARR,[4] the third daughter of GABRIEL BARR,[3] married WILLIAM RICHIE STEWART October 20, 1853. They live at Paxton, Illinois. He is a ruling elder in the United Presbyterian Church at Paxton. There were born to them six children.

1 Infant son, born July 22, 1854, and died the same day.

2 ANNA ELIZABETH STEWART,[5] born July 22, 1854, and died January 20, 1884.

3 THOMAS MORTON STEWART,[5] born December 26, 1861, died September 21, 1864.

4 Infant son, born May 14, 1864, died the same day.

5 JOHN TRUESDALE STEWART.[5]

6 MARTHA REBECCA STEWART.[5]

5 JOHN TRUESDALE STEWART.[5]

5 JOHN TRUESDALE STEWART[5] was born January 13, 1868. He was married to IDA BELLE WILSON January 1, 1900. He is a civil engineer and engaged in government surveys in the Black Hills and Northwestern States. He spent last winter (1899) in Washington, D. C., mapping his work. He is reported as a very sagacious business man, and a man of excellent character and unimpeachable integrity.

6 MARTHA REBECCA STEWART.[5]

6 MARTHA REBECCA STEWART[5] was born May 2, 1872. She is a graduate of the nurse's training school, Chicago, Illinois. She was married September 26, 1900, to Dr. NORMAN PERRY MILLS. Their home will be at Appleton, Wisconsin.

6 ELIZABETH BARR.[4]

6 ELIZABETH BARR[4] was born October 8, 1838. She married JAMES BRISBIN February 3, 1857. He was born January 8, 1834. Seven children were born to them.

    1 MARY ANN BRISBIN,[5] born November 15, 1859, died November 14, 1887.

    2 EMMA M. BRISBIN.[5]

    3 ALICE JANE BRISBIN.[5]

    4 Infant son, born November 16, 1857, died same day.

    5 Infant son, born August 12, 1858.

    6 Infant daughter, born February 15, 1862.

    7 Infant son, born July 1, 1869.

2 EMMA M. BRISBIN.[5]

2 EMMA M. BRISBIN[5] was born August 24, 1863. She married Mr. FRANK YOST February 1, 1883. They have one son. RALPH YOST[6] was born October 6, 1893.

3 ALICE JANE BRISBIN.[5]

3 ALICE JANE BRISBIN[5] was born December 12, 1875. She married FRANK P. MILLER April 7, 1894. They have three children.

    DWIGHT P. MILLER,[6] born February 3, 1895.

    RAY BRISBIN MILLER,[6] born September 5, 1897.

    EMMA MILLER,[6] born January 5, 1900.

7 REBECCA ANN BARR.[4]

7 REBECCA ĀNN BARR,[4] was born June 13, 1841. She married JOHN A. KENNEDY December 2, 1858. She died July 2, 1878. They had three children.

Infant daughter, born and died October 25, 1859.

JAMES PRESTON KENNEDY[5] was born August 11, 1861. He married IDA KATE DILGER September 13, 1885. They have no family.

SAMUEL BARR KENNEDY[5] was born December 26, 1866. He married MARY BELL TURNER in April, 1895. They have no family.

8 ROBERT McTEER BARR.[4]

8 ROBERT McTEER BARR,[4] youngest son of GABRIEL BARR,[3] was born December 7, 1843, and died April 14, 1898. He married SUSAN E. BAKER October 16, 1866. She was born March 23, 1848. To this union were born five children.

1 SARAH M. BARR.[5]
2 ANNA L. BARR.[5]
3 DANIEL M. BARR.[5]
4 MAMIE BARR.[5]
5 Infant, deceased.

1 SARAH M. BARR.[5]

1 SARAH M. BARR[5] was born May 11, 1868. She married Mr. W. F. LENTZ December 28, 1891. They have two children. Their present address is Piqua, Ohio.

FLORENCE LEE LENTZ.[6]
PAULINE B. LENTZ.[6]

2 ANNA L. BARR.[5]

2 ANNA L. BARR[5] was born March 15, 1871, and died August 26, 1893.

3 DANIEL M. BARR.[5]

3 DANIEL M. BARR[5] was born October 6, 1875. He is unmarried and is an attorney at Somerset, Ohio. His father, Robert McTeer Barr, was a prominent attorney in Somerset, Ohio, for years.

They are members of the Methodist Episcopal Church.

4 MAMIE BARR.[5]

4 MAMIE BARR[5] was born January 28, 1878. She was married to DAVID T. FRY November 20, 1898. Their home is New Lexington, Ohio. They have one child, ROBERT WILLIAM FRY.[6]

There are thirty-four grandchildren of Gabriel Barr.[3]

This closes the family record of GABRIEL BARR,[2] fifth son of ROBERT BARR.[1] This family has a good record for religious convictions and faithfulness to principle. They are mostly members of the United Presbyterian Church.

We are sorry not to have a more complete report of some of the families of this branch, but we have done the best we could.

In this family there are 236 members: two lawyers, one minister, and five who took part in the Civil War. In every way they are a credit to the name. And although it is one of the largest families, so far as we know there is not a "black sheep" among them.

FAMILY VI.

MARGARET BARR.[2]

The last member of the family of ROBERT BARR,[1] our great-grandfather, was a daughter by the name of MARGARET.[2] She was born October 11, 1764, in Ireland. She came with the rest of the family to America in 1790. She died July 17, 1795, after an illness of nineteen days. She never married, and died at the home of her father, near McAlevy's Fort, Pennsylvania.

Her brother Samuel in his memoirs writes of her: "She lived without pride or affectation, and peacefully fell asleep in the hope of a better resurrection and a glorious immortality."

This closes the record of the descendants of ROBERT BARR,[1] covering six generations.

FINIS.

In concluding this history, we may say the blessing of God has rested upon our noble ancestor RÓBERT BARR,[1] and his descendants, from the time he left Ireland till this present time. They have multiplied and replenished the earth, being remarkable for their large families.

They have not forgotten the Covenant of God, being generally religious and connected with some branch of the great Christian Church.

They have occupied for the most part a middle place in their respective communities, being of that class which were respected for their Christian integrity and industrious, thrifty habits.

They passed through many struggles and difficulties, but possessed the courage and determination necessary to overcome, and so have held their own with their fellows and have left behind them an influence for good more lasting than marble shaft or granite pillar.

The Rev. John M. Adair, who for thirty years was pastor of the Stone Valley United Presbyterian Church (from 1859 to 1889)—of which our Great-grandfather Robert Barr[1] and his son Samuel were among the founders, and which was the church of all the Barr families in that valley—says of them :

"The Barr families had the usual characteristics of the Scotch-Irish, an unusual rigidity and firmness of character, and were ever ready to stand for what they regarded as true and right, whatever others might think of them, and however much it might affect their secular interests. They were intelligent and quite enterprising, and made useful members of the Christian church and of society."

After perusing such a history, one cannot but be impressed with the thought of the far-reaching influence of a single family, as you trace it down through several generations, and mark the results of the careful home-training of the children in the love of truth and virtue, and the inculcation of righteous principles and noble aspirations in their young hearts, which fits them for the society and citizenship both of earth and heaven.

It is like the waves of the sea started by a single pebble, which roll on until they touch the farthest shore. So is the influence of human life for evil or for good.

While we cannot absolutely predict the future of a family, and the part it may act on life's great stage, or the place it may occupy in human history, we can say to our dear relatives and friends, that we need have no fear of the future for ourselves or the generations that are to follow,—amid the rapidly changing conditions both in state and church,—if we will but put on the whole armor of God, spoken of so minutely by the great apostle Paul in Ephesians 6:10-18.

Bearing the fruits of the Spirit, and putting off the works of darkness, we can safely cast ourselves upon the mercy and care of the Great Pilot of the Galilean Lake, who knows the sea and is master of the waves, and who will bring us safely into the haven of rest and peace, a reunited family in heaven. In so doing we but imitate our worthy ancestors, and shall be able to build upon the granite foundations which they have laid, in the eternal principles of righteousness, for coming generations.

I confess to a feeling of deep anxiety for our children and the rising generation, that the culture of soul, as well as of body and mind; that Christian principles, as well as a knowledge of the arts and sciences, receive that attention and occupy that place in their lives and learning, to which they are justly entitled as being of supreme importance. No life is valuable to the world or to God without it. The question of our Saviour is the one unanswerable question:

"What is a man profited if he should gain the whole world and lose his own soul; or what shall he give in exchange for his soul?"

We make the most of time and life when we build for eternity—when we fulfil the great mission of our creation; namely, "to glorify God and to enjoy him forever."

"Reflect that life, like ev'ry other blessing,
Derives its value from its use alone."

May we all prepare to meet on the brighter shores, and in that better country.

NOTICE.

We hope the friends will be careful to make corrections, where mistakes occur, on the appended blank pages for that purpose. Also, please inform the writer of this book of the same as soon as discovered.

There are also pages for additional record of the families, that it may be kept together for easy reference.

SUPPLEMENT.

LOTTIE A. BARR.[6]
(See page 30.)

LOTTIE A. BARR,[6] daughter of LEMUEL C. and Maria J. Johnston Barr, married Mr. WILLIAM R. WRIGHT October 20, 1896. He was born May 17, 1874. They had two children. The oldest is dead. The name of the second is—

HERSCHEL L. WRIGHT,[7] born October 24, 1898.

Their address is Sabetha, Kansas.

JOHN H. BARR.[6]
(See page 30.)

JOHN H. BARR,[6] brother of Lottie Barr, was married February 4, 1896, to ELVIRA GAGE. She was born February 25, 1876. They have two children.

LOTTIE A. BARR,[7] born December 5, 1896.

MURMLON M. BARR,[7] born February 25, 1898.

Their address is. Woodlawn, Kansas.

Mr. HOWARD FOSTER BARR'S[5] youngest child's name is WILLIAM DALE BARR.[6] They live at Dakota, Illinois. (See page 31.)

3 JOHN D. CUMMINS.[5]
(See page 35.)

3 Mr. JOHN D. CUMMINS[5] enlisted in the Sixth Regiment United States Volunteer Cavalry as a private, October 27, 1862, and was honorably discharged November 21, 1864, having served in twenty different engagements.

He was taken prisoner at Funkstown, Maryland, July 7, 1863, and remained in the hands of the enemy at Andersonville prison until exchanged in November, 1863.

He was in three of General Sheridan's raids: Berryville, Manchester and Cedar Creek.

Four children were born to them.

MARY CATHARINE CUMMINS,[6] born at Lake City, Minnesota, December 21, 1872, died January 1, 1874.

CARRIE MAY CUMMINS,[6] born at Rockelm, Pierce County, Wisconsin, is living at home.

WILLIAM BEATTY CUMMINS,[6] born at Lake City, Minnesota, September 17, 1875. He is a stationary engineer, and works at Eldora, Iowa.

EMMA RIGHLEY CUMMINS,[6] born at Lake City, Minnesota, April 8, 1877.

---

2 JENNIE D. STEWART.[5]
(See page 37.)

2 JENNIE D. STEWART[5] was born June 15, 1852, and was married November 4, 1869. To her were born the following children :

MAUDE BAKER,[6] born September 15, 1870, now living in Des Moines, Iowa.

BESSIE BAKER,[6] born April 10, 1872, died September 4, 1879.

IDA BAKER,[6] born August 1, 1876, is at home.

BESSIE BAKER,[6] born March 25, 1874, died September 8, 1879.

FLOYD BAKER,[6] born October 13, 1882, is at home.

They are all members of the Presbyterian Church of Cedarville, Illinois.

IV SAMUEL BARR.[3]
(See page 81.)

4 SAMUEL BARR[3] married Miss SUSAN EVERHART, a daughter of Samuel Everhart. To them were born five children, two sons and three daughters. Two of the daughters died young. The three living are—

1 MARTHA BARR.[4] She married JOHN BEAUMONT, and died in Clearfield County, Pennsylvania

2 SAMUEL E. BARR.[4] (See pages 81 and 137.)

3 DAVID BARR.[4]

3 DAVID BARR.[4]

3 DAVID BARR[4] was born in Center County, Pennsylvania, in 1815. He died after a long illness, in Mifflin County, in January, 1889, aged seventy-four years, and was buried beside his wife at Kelly Presbyterian Church.

He married ELIZABETH ZONES, of Lycoming County, Pennsylvania. They lived in Center County, near Boalsburg, until after the war. He sold out and moved to Franklinville, Huntingdon County, Pennsylvania. They lived there for nearly ten years, then moved to Philipsburg, Center County, Pennsylvania, and from thence to Mifflin County, in 1879 or 1880, where he died.

To them were born eight children, seven of whom are living.

MARY JANE BARR.[5] She married JOHN METZ, of Mill Creek, Huntingdon County, Pennsylvania. He is dead, and she makes her home with her son, at Yeagertown, Mifflin County, Pennsylvania.

SAMUEL EVERHART BARR[5] was in the Civil War.

JOHN M. CLAYTON BARR[5] married Miss TOMELSON, of Huntingdon County, Pennsylvania. They live at Yeagertown, Pennsylvania. He is employed in the steel works there. He was in the Civil War.

SUSANNAH BARR[5] married THOMAS Gates, and resides at
Mill Creek, Huntingdon County, Pennsylvania.

SARAH IRVIN BARR[5] married Mr. GOWLAND. Where
they live we have not been able to learn.

BENJAMIN EVERHART BARR[5] lives in Yeagertown and
works in the steel works there.

MITCHELL BARR[5] is also employed at the steel works at
Yeagertown.

Mr. SAMUEL BARR[3] died, and his widow married JOHN
SPARR. She died in 1849. Her second daughter, ELLEN
SPARR, married Mr. THOMPSON BARR.[4] (See page 72.)

---

3 MRS. JANE A. BARR[4] died February 7, 1901, at her
home in Carthage, Illinois. She died of a combination of
diseases, in the full assurance of faith. She sat up a while on
the morning of the day she died, but said: "I feel as if the
end was near, and I am ready and anxious to go and be at rest."
(See page 67 also 142.)

---

2 J. M. WASSON[5] married Miss EUGENIA LeCOMTE December 8, 1879, at Meadville, Pennsylvania. She was the daughter
of Anatol and Mary LeComte. She died May 9, 1894. They
moved to Fostoria, Ohio, in November, 1887, where Mr.
Wasson and family still live. He is engaged in the oil and gas
business. He has four children.

RACHEL WASSON,[6] born October 30, 1880.

WILLIAM A. WASSON,[6] born September 8, 1882.

MARSHALL J. WASSON,[6] born July 17, 1884.

EMMA WASSON,[6] born June 14, 1886.

(See page 64.)

---

2 MAHALA ANN BARR[4] was born May 26, 1818. She
was married to WASHINGTON TAYLOR March 13, 1834, and

died when about thirty years old, leaving one son by the name of DAVID JACKSON TAYLOR. (See page 60.)

MARY MILLER.[4]
(See page 82.)

MARY MILLER,[4] eldest daughter of Margaret (Barr) MILLER,[3] and granddaughter of David Barr,[2] married JOHN HARTSWICK, of Boalsburg, Pennsylvania. To them were born four children.

  1 HARVEY HARTSWICK.[5]
  2 WESTLEY HARTSWICK.[5]
  3 ADAM HARTSWICK.[5]
  4 MARY HARTSWICK.[5]

1 HARRY HARTSWICK.[5]

  1 HARRY HARTSWICK married LYDIA PRICE, at Boalsburg. He was a farmer and a Democrat.

2 WESTLEY HARTSWICK.[5]

  2 WESTLY HEARTSWICK[5] is married, and lived for a time at East Brady, Pennsylvania. He lives now in Allegheny City, Pennsylvania. He is a merchant, and owns one of the largest grocery stores in the city. In politics he is a Republican. They are all members of the Presbyterian Church. They have four children.

  ——— HARTSWICK.[6]
  CURTIS HARTSWICK.[6]
  ALBERT HARTSWICK.[6]
  MAY HARTSWICK.[6]

3 ADAM HARTSWICK.[5]

  3 ADAM HARTSWICK[5] married twice. He had two children by the first wife. He was a Republican. He died at Altoona.

JENNIE HARTSWICK[6] married FRANK TORRENCE. She died of cancer of the throat. She left two sons. Mr. Torrence married again, and lives in Punxsutawney. He is a merchant.

FRANK HARTSWICK.[6]

Mr. Adam Hartswick's second wife lives in Punxsutawney.

4 MARY HARTSWICK.[5]

4 MARY HARTSWICK[5] married CHRISTIAN HARTSWICK. He is a blacksmith. In politics he is a Republican. To them were born five children.

   1 ADAM HARTSWICK.[6]
   2 JOHN HARTSWICK.[6]
   3 MARGARET HARTSWICK.[6]
   4 HENRY HARTSWICK.[6]
   5 JANE HARTSWICK.[6]

1 ADAM HARTSWICK.[6]

1 ADAM HARTSWICK[6] married SALLIE MOTHERSBAUGH. He was a farmer. They moved to Altoona, Pennsylvania, and he died there in 1898. She is still living in Altoona. To them were born seven children.

   ELEANOR HARTSWICK[7] is married and lives in Altoona.

   ELIZABETH HARTSWICK[7] is married, and lived and died in Altoona. She left two children, a boy and a girl.

   JOHN HARTSWICK[7] is at home with his mother, in Altoona.

   JANE HARTSWICK[7] is married and lives in Harrisburg.

   MACK HARTSWICK[7] is at home.

   EDITH HARTSWICK[7] is at home.

   LIZZIE HARTSWICK[7] died in Altoona.

2 JOHN HARTSWICK, M. D.[6]

2 JOHN HARTSWICK, M. D.,[6] was married in 1872, to KATE HUSTON. They live in Clearfield, Pennsylvania. He is

one of the best physicians in the county, and has been very successful. He is wealthy and has a fine home. He is an elder in the Presbyterian Church. They have three children.

HUSTON HARTSWICK, M. D.,[7] was a young physician. He graduated from the Medical University of Pennsylvania. He was two years at West Point, but it was too heavy for him, and he turned his attention to medicine. After he was through with his studies he broke down in health and went south and practiced one year; came home and went to Colorado, and then to Mexico, where he died of consumption. He was very tall, fine looking, and a perfect gentleman.

ELIZABETH HARTSWICK[7] married WILLIAM IRVIN, a lawyer in Clearfield, and they are living there at present. The Irvins are a prominent family in the county.

HOWARD HARTSWICK[7] married Miss JENNIE BETZ, daughter of Senator Betz of Clearfield County, a very wealthy and prominent family. Her father has been State senator from that district for years. Howard Hartswick was State librarian under Governor Hastings. They have two boys.

3 MARGARET HARTSWICK.[6]

3 MARGARET HARTSWICK[6] married HENRY EVEY and lives on the Hartswick farm. He served throughout the Civil War, and had a good war record. He is a Republican. They live near Pennsylvania State College, Center County. She died at Boalsburg, Center County, Pennsylvania. They had six children.

ELIZABETH EVEY[7] married ANDY HOUSEMAN. They live in Altoona Pennsylvania.

JOHN EVEY[7] married, and lives in Altoona.

CHRISTIAN EVEY[7] married, and lives in Altoona.

WILLIAM EVEY.[7]

ALLISON EVEY[7] married, and lives in Lewiston.

MARGARET EVEY[7] married Mr. LOVE, and lives in Pittsburg, Pennsylvania.

4 HENRY HARTSWICK.[6]

4 HENRY HARTSWICK[6] was a school-teacher and a smart man. He is married and has four children. They live near the State College.

CLARA ELIZABETH[7] died a few months before her graduation. She was a bright, promising girl.

JOHN HARTSWICK[7] lives at home. He is a teacher.

NEWTON HARTSWICK[7] is at home.

5 JANE HARTSWICK.[6]

5 JANE HARTSWICK[6] never married. She lived on the farm for years, and then made her home with her Aunt Betsy till she died. She then made her home with Dr. John Hartswick, and died there. She was one of the salt of the earth.

VI POLLY BARR.[3]
(See page 81.)

POLLY BARR[3] had five children, instead of three.

1 SARAH McCORMICK.[4]

2 MARGARET McCORMICK.[4]

3 JANE McCORMICK.[4]

4 GEORGE McCORMICK.[4]

5 JAMES McCORMICK.[4]

1 SARAH McCORMICK.[4]

1 SARAH McCORMICK[4] married DANIEL RILEY, and lived near Boalsburg, Center County, Pennsylvania, all their lives. She was born in 1806, and died in 1882, at the age of seventy-six. Mr. Riley died in 1873. They had twelve children—seven sons and five daughters.

JAMES M. RILEY[5] was married to Miss CATHERINE SPARR, and lived near Boalsburg. Mr. Riley died in Indiana some years ago, and Mrs. Riley makes her home with her two daughters, Florence and Sarah, who married men by the name of McCormick.

DANIEL RILEY[5] was killed in the Civil War. He was single.

GEORGE RILEY[5] was also killed in the Civil War. He was married, and left one daughter, who married Mr. SANDOW and lives at Center Hall, Center County, Pennsylvania.

REBECCA RILEY[5] married EDWARD KRAMER. They have four children, all born in Boalsburg.

> SARAH KRAMER[6] married THOMAS HUNTER, of Boalsburg. He died some years ago.
>
> ANDREW KRAMER[6] married Miss CLARA CONDO. They live in Johnstown, Pennsylvania, where her father and mother also live.
>
> MARY KRAMER[6] married HENRY KENNEDY, who lost his life in the Johnstown flood in 1889. Mrs. Kennedy now resides in Philadelphia with her five children.
>
> DANIEL RILEY KRAMER[6] married in Johnstown, and died there some years ago.

THOMAS RILEY[5] married MARGARET SECKLER. They have two daughters and one son, all living in Boalsburg.

JANE RILEY[5] married J. GRUM IRWIN. They live at Oak Hall, Center County, Pennsylvania. They have two daughters.

> ANNIE IRWIN[6] married WILLIAM MITCHELL.
>
> LECRESIA IRWIN[6] married THOMAS JOHNSTON, of Hollidaysburg, Pennsylvania.

SARAH RILEY[5] married DUNCAN RANKIN. They have one daughter.

BELLE RANKIN[6] married EDWARD McINTIRE, of Altoona, Pennsylvania.

WILLIAM RILEY[5] lives in Chicago.

CALVIN RILEY[5] lives with his sister, Mrs. Rankin, in Boalsburg.

MARTHA RILEY,[5] the youngest daughter, married ALEXANDER EVERHART in 1875. They live at 802 Lexington Avenue, Altoona, Pennsylvania.

MARGARET BARR McCORMICK.[4]
(See page 81.)

MARGARET McCORMICK[4] married Mr. WILLIAM MILLER. They had three children, two sons and one daughter.

GEORGE McCORMICK[5] was married and lived and died in Crawford County, Pennsylvania.

JAMES McCORMICK[5] died when quite young.

VIII MARGARET BARR.[3]
(See page 81.)

8 MARGARET BARR,[3] who married ADAM MILLER, had four sons and two daughters.

HARRY MILLER[4] is still living at Boalsburg, but very feeble.

WESLEY MILLER.[4]

ADAM MILLER.[4]

THOMPSON MILLER.[4]

JANE MILLER.[4]

MARY MILLER.[4]

Mrs. Miller died on the old Barr homestead, near Boalsburg, in 1843.

GEORGE M. BARR.[4]
(See page 113.)

They have three children.

GEORGIE ETTA BARR[5] was born at Lewisburg, Pennsylvania, July 6, 1884.

CARROLL SAMUEL SCOTT BARR[5] was born at Delmar, Delaware, March 10, 1887.

MARY HELEN BARR[5] was born at Delmar, Delaware, March 25, 1891.

Mr. Barr owns a fine home in Delmar, and has a pleasant family.

---

2 CLINTON BARR WINTERSTEIN.[5]
(See page 156.)

2 CLINTON B. WINTERSTEIN[5] was born August 26, 1842. He is single. He enlisted in the Union Army, in Company C, 64th Regiment Ohio Volunteer Infantry, known as the Sherman Brigade, on October 4, 1861. He began active service at Louisville, Kentucky. He experienced some hard campaigning and fighting, being in the battles of Chickamauga, Missionary Ridge, and Lookout Mountain. At the close of three years' service he reenlisted January 1, 1864, as a veteran. He went from Columbus, Ohio, to Nashville, Tennessee, and from there to Chattanooga, where they started May 3, 1864, on the campaign to Atlanta, Georgia. They were one hundred and twenty days under fire. There was not a day that they did not hear the bullets whistling. He was wounded slightly in the charge on Rockyface Ridge, May 9, 1864, which laid him aside for one week. At the close of this campaign they returned to Nashville, Tennessee. His command was sent to Louisiana, and then to Texas at the close of the war. He has a grand war record. He was mustered out December 3, 1865, having

served four years and three months. He moved to Dakota in March, 1900.

His mother, Jane (Barr) Winterstein, died February 14, 1844. His father died in 1883.

9 MARY BARR.[4]

9 MARY BARR[4] is the daughter of DAVID and RACHAEL (PAXTON) BARR (see page 59). She was born January 27, 1826. She was married twice. Her first husband was JOHN CONN. They were married May 29, 1845. Mr. Conn was born April 21, 1818, and died October 5, 1883.

Mrs. Conn was married to GEORGE G. GIBSON March 28, 1888. He was born January 13, 1819. He died April 13, 1899. She had no children by either husband. She lives at Shira, Butler County, Pennsylvania.

6 ELIZABETH BARR.[4]
(See page 58.)

The names of Mr. J. J CORBETT's family are as follows:

JAMES R. CORBETT,[5] born April 24, 1834.
ROBERT BARR CORBETT,[5] born June 9, 1836.
ISAIAH CORBETT,[5] born February 12, 1838.
MARY ELIZABETH CORBETT,[5] born July 22, 1840.
SARAH CATHARINE CORBETT,[5] born April 22, 1843.
LEWIS CORBETT,[5] born August 17, 1845.
CENITH CORBETT,[5] born SEPTEMBER 20, 1846.
WILLIAM BLADEN CORBETT,[5] born March 20, 1849.
LORETTA CORBETT,[5] born July 22, 1851.
LAWRENCE CORBETT,[5] born August 21, 1854.
Infant, born June 16, 1857, and died the same day.

James R. Corbett enlisted September, 1861, for service in the Civil War. Isaiah enlisted in 1863. Robert was drafted in 1864. They were all discharged in 1865.

INDEX.

The index is arranged alphabetically by families, for easy reference. (See page 9.)

Great-grandfather Robert Barr.

FAMILY I. (See page 17.)

FAMILY II. (See page 55.)

FAMILY III. (See page 83.)

FAMILY IV. (See page 84.)

FAMILY V.   (See page 155.)

FAMILY VI. (See page 180.)

CORRECTIONS.

ADDITIONS.

ADDITIONS.

ADDITIONS.

Lightning Source UK Ltd.
Milton Keynes UK
UKHW020638090223
416652UK00001B/241